Ara Mai He Tētēkura – Visioning Our Futures

*The Māori title, 'Ara Mai He Tētēkura', comes from the whakataukī
'Mate atu he tētē kura, ara mai he tētē kura' – 'When the fern frond
dies, another rises in its place.'*

*In its entirety this proverb metaphorically encapsulates Māori
leadership – the first part, 'Mate atu he tētēkura', acknowledging
historical figures who have led Māoridom through the challenges
of their time and the second, 'Ara mai he tētē kura', describing
the emergence of new leaders in response to contemporary issues.*

James Ataria

Ara Mai He Tētēkura – Visioning Our Futures

New and emerging pathways of Māori academic leadership

Edited by

*Paul Whitinui, Marewa Glover
and Dan Hikuroa*

OTAGO

Published by Otago University Press
PO Box 56 / Level 1, 398 Cumberland Street
Dunedin, New Zealand
university.press@otago.ac.nz
www.otago.ac.nz/press

First published 2013
Text copyright © the contributors as named 2013
Volume copyright © Otago University Press 2013

The moral rights of the authors have been asserted.
ISBN 978-1-877578-60-1

Published with the assistance of Te Manu Ao Academy

Publisher: Rachel Scott
Editor: Ross Calman

Cover artwork: Ani Kainamu

Printed in New Zealand by PrintStop Ltd, Wellington

Contents

Acknowledgements

The authors of *Ara Mai He Tētēkura – Visioning our Futures: New and emerging pathways of Māori academic leadership* wish to thank the following individuals and organisations:

The various academic and research-based institutions and organisations for providing the time, support and resources for contributors to write their chapters.

Te Manu Ao Academy (a national inter-university Māori academy for academic and professional advancement) Massey University, for sponsoring the book project.

All the reviewers who provided supportive and constructive feedback.

Ani Kainamu (PhD candidate, University of Canterbury) for the cover artwork.

James Ataria (Lincoln University) for providing the title and explanation.

Staff at Otago University Press.

The future Māori academic leaders who will emerge from a wide range of different disciplines and scholarly backgrounds.

Finally, all our family and friends without whose ongoing love, support and encouragement this book would never have eventuated.

Ngā mihi nui ki a koutou katoa!

Readers' comments on this book

Ara Mai He Tētēkura - Visioning our Futures provides a wide range of views about Māori academic leadership in modern times. It is a significant publication that gives just cause for optimism not only for Māori futures but also for a new wave of Māori leaders who have the obvious capacity to take Māori aspirations to unprecedented heights. It is clear from each chapter that tomorrow's leaders will have deep knowledge of a range of subjects and methodologies and will be able to straddle the interface between academic disciplines and Māori values, knowledge and world views. Thinking in two dimensions and ascribing to dual perspectives will be a matter of course.

But the more significant contribution of *Ara Mai He Tētēkura* lies in the potential for collective leadership. By bringing together individual views and perspectives, the prospect of collaboration between leaders from different persuasions becomes apparent. While each chapter contains a unique viewpoint, together they highlight the breadth of Māori academic leadership, united by a common commitment to Māori and by a shared belief that teaching and research need not be constrained by a single tradition. Māori academic leadership is moving away from charismatic leaders who often had little option than to work in isolation from each other, towards a type of leadership that is networked, distributed, sustainable and strategic.

In that respect Manu Ao has been an important catalyst for Māori leadership networks. By creating a forum that goes beyond disciplinary silos and fosters collective creativity, it has shown that *he toa takatini* is both achievable and effective. *Ara Mai He Tētēkura* is further evidence of the breadth and sustainability of a new generation of Māori leaders.

Mason Durie KNZM

In Coast Salish tradition, I raise my hands in thanks and respect to the editors, Paul Whitinui, Marewa Glover and Dan Hikuroa, for their ground-breaking book, *Ara Mai He Tētēkura*. The Indigenous peoples on the west coast of British Columbia, Canada, and the Māori of Aotearoa have had longstanding academic relationships for many years. This commentary continues the learning relationship between our respective countries.

We are at a critical juncture at tertiary institutions or universities where the very few seasoned Indigenous academics are reaching retirement. Unfortunately, there are only a few Indigenous associate professors and even fewer full professors at Canadian universities. Now is the time to better prepare Indigenous doctoral candidates, assistant, and associate professors for the additional leadership responsibilities they will have in academe.

Ara Mai He Tētēkura is an important learning tool for this purpose. The multi-disciplinary Indigenous editors and authors of this book not only share thoughtful and thought-provoking stories, struggles and successes related to academic leadership; they have created strong, clear and vibrant pathways upon which to travel.

Jo-ann Archibald
Q'um Q'um Xiiem
University of British Columbia

If there were any characteristics that would distinguish a rangatira from a leader, they would be those that we would recognise as tika, pono and aroha. Each of the contributors in their own unique way reminds us that a Māori leader is one whose values are rooted firmly in the past but whose practice as an academic is focused on the future.

Moreover, that future is one characterised by those duties that are to be found in the relationship between tuakana and teina. And while the uninformed outsider might describe that relationship as one characterised by duty and responsibility, and consequently burdensome, we would recognise the relationship as one of huge satisfaction and reward.

Such is the message provided in this book by our new and emerging Māori academic leaders. I commend them for their contribution to building a Māori academy and have no doubt that in so doing they will make it easier for those who follow to walk in their footsteps.

Associate Professor Pare Keiha
Pro-Vice Chancellor Māori Advancement
Pro-Vice Chancellor Learning and Teaching
Dean/Tumuaki Te Ara Poutama/Faculty of Māori Development, AUT University

Foreword

It is often said that the primary role of any academic is to act as the conscience of society. For Māori academics there is an added responsibility: to play a pivotal role in transforming the society they belong to. The need to transform Te Ao Māori stems from a history of colonisation, which now contributes towards Māori occupying most, if not all, negative socio-economic statistics. Most research undertaken by Māori academics, in some way, shape or form, ultimately contributes towards adding understanding regarding an issue that affects Māori. Equally, their teachings are aimed towards providing students with knowledge and tools that will provide insight into the Māori world. Māori academics act as transformative agents for the communities they serve.

Being a transformative agent also requires Māori academics to be equipped with a different skill set. Māori academics walk in two worlds: Te Ao Māori and academia. Historically the two environments have not been complementary. The Western convention of separating the researcher from the researched and the non-validation of Māori knowledge by Western academics has given rise to continuing debates that have seen Māori academics pitted against Western academic purists. Despite the emergence over a relatively short period of time of Western-trained Māori academics and, over an even shorter period of time, of Māori academics who have challenged historical Western research dogma, the debate over appropriate research methodologies involving Māori has swung in favour of Māori academics.

Accompanying the debate over appropriate research methodologies when interacting with Māori has been the rise of Māori-originated frameworks and principles to explain phenomena. Generic Māori principles such as whakawhanaungatanga (making connections), manaakitanga (caring for the people), rangatiratanga (chieftainship) and kaitiakitanga (guardianship) now underpin approaches to and analyses of research concerning Māori.

The use by Māori academics of a Māori lens by which to view the world is now commonplace and highlights the quantum leap undertaken over the past generation or so in the field of research. Notwithstanding the advances made by Māori academics in recent years, there still exist many challenging issues for Māori within academia. Perhaps above all else, the main challenge for Māori academics is the lack of critical mass.

Great strides have been made in increasing the number of Māori doctoral graduates but Māori remain under-represented when considering the proportion of Māori within New Zealand's population. The number of Māori doctoral graduates needs to increase and the need is more pronounced when contemplating the projected rise in the Māori population over the next 25 years. Coupled with the need to increase the number of Māori graduates is the challenge presented by the retirement of leading Māori academics. Over the past decade Emeritus Professors Ranginui Walker and Sir Mason Durie have retired, although they remain active in various leadership roles in their communities. They undoubtedly leave behind a long and proud legacy of academic work that will continue to serve not only Māoridom, but also future generations of New Zealanders. There can be no denying, however, that their departure has created a void and the need for leadership succession.

Ara Mai He Tētēkura – Visioning Our Futures is a collection of writing by emerging Māori academics that records and communicates both advances and challenges for new and emerging Māori academics. This book provides a valuable insight to anyone who is interested in the plight of Māori academics today. The chapters have been penned by Māori academics who are establishing themselves as the next generation of Māori academic leaders. As such, they will become more influential within society and on the future of New Zealand as their careers progress.

The wide variety of disciplines the contributors for this publication specialise within is worth noting and celebrating. Eight contributors work within the field of health, five within the environment, two within education, and one within art. Historically, Māori academics have been strictly located within the discipline of Māori Studies. This publication demonstrates that Māori academics are now situated within a number of different specialist disciplines, and are established and recognised within their respective fields of study.

My involvement with this publication stems from a leadership wānanga that I facilitated in 2011. Hosted by Manu Ao: A National Inter-University Māori Academy for Academic and Professional Advancement, a discussion was held among the participants about the issues, challenges and opportunities they were encountering within their own tertiary institutions. It was agreed at the wānanga that there is a need to articulate, document and share their experiences with the wider academic community. The wānanga also illustrated the need for Māori academics to meet on a regular basis. The opportunity to impart experiences was valuable for participants and the opportunity to network and build stronger relationships with one another has led to collaborative projects, such as this publication.

Regular forums for Māori academics should be encouraged by tertiary institutions as the need to support more Māori in pursuing academic careers becomes greater. In the years ahead, Māori academics will face new challenges and opportunities. Much like their predecessors, the current band of Māori academics will encounter changing societal contexts that will pose threats as well as offer prospects for Māori. In the post-World War II era, the age of urbanisation saw the Māori populace shift from living in rural communities to urban centres. Accompanying this shift was a number of associated challenges: a young Māori population disconnected from their tribal base; the emergence of Māori-based gangs; the creation of predominantly Māori and Pacific Island communities within state-sector housing estates; and the rise of low-wage Māori employment within factory-based industries.

In today's environment, Māori face a multitude of challenges in the digital age. Recent research strongly suggests that in the future more Māori will live away from their tribal lands and that technology will be vital in maintaining linkages, that the Māori workforce will need to be further educated to participate within a knowledge economy, and that innovative schemes will have to be explored by both the Crown and iwi to raise the current socio-economic position of Māori. Māori academics are armed with the tools required to address the issues Māori will encounter. Many of the contributors to this publication conduct research that focuses on Māori issues that require academic attention. What is imperative in the search for Māori-based solutions is the nurturing and growth of emerging Māori academics. *Ara Mai He Tētēkura – Visioning Our Futures* is the first step towards achieving that goal.

Malcolm Mulholland
Ngāti Kahungunu ki Wairarapa
Facilitator
Manu Ao Academy

Preface

Ka pū te ruha, ka hao te rangatahi.

As an old net withers a new one is made (when an elder is no longer able to lead, a younger leader will stand in his place).

As this book shows, emerging Māori academic leaders have much to say about what leadership should look like in the future. If we are to have effective academic leaders in the future, we must identify them now and provide them with leadership development opportunities. That is what we set out to do with Manu Ao.

As New Zealand becomes increasingly exposed to global competitiveness there will be a need for well-qualified, high-calibre Māori academic leadership. In order to attain high levels of professionalism and continuing professional development, an active link between academic leadership and the wider dimensions of Māori social, cultural and economic advancement will be essential. However, despite a rapidly growing cadre of Māori graduates who possess doctoral qualifications, there remains a relative lack of Māori in senior academic positions, to the extent that a potential leadership crisis exists.

Te Kāhui Amokura, Universities New Zealand's Māori committee, was concerned that the leadership profile was in flux. As a consequence, it applied to the Tertiary Education Commission for funding and was successful in securing a three-year contract to establish the Manu Ao Academy. The Manu Ao Academy was a national inter-university Māori academy for academic and professional advancement, supported by Universities New Zealand in association with all eight New Zealand universities. Te Kāhui Amokura acted as the governance entity for this programme, which was hosted by Massey University between 2008 and 2011. The academy had a three fold aim of accelerating Māori leadership, advancing Māori scholarship, and strengthening links between Māori professionals and Māori academics. The academy organised a range of activities to achieve these aims, including leadership wānanga for emerging Māori academics.

The idea of a book about Māori academic leadership stemmed from a discussion among a number of emerging Māori academic leaders at an inter-university leadership wānanga run by the Manu Ao Academy at Waiwhetū Marae, Lower Hutt, in September 2011. The seed had been planted by the inspirational wānanga presentations from senior academic leaders, including Emeritus Professor Sir Mason Durie ('A day in the life of a senior leader in a university'), Professor Margaret Mutu ('Staying balanced: Māori community versus the academy') and Professor Wally Penetito ('My journey to professorship'). Led by Dr Paul Whitinui, their unbridled enthusiasm for the project knew no bounds, particularly when the Manu Ao Academy accepted the challenge to sponsor the two-year venture. *Ara Mai He Tētēkura – Visioning our Futures: New and emerging pathways of Māori academic leadership* reflects the experiences and points of view of 13 emerging Māori academics from tertiary education institutions across Aotearoa.

This book is one of a series of Manu Ao legacy publications that includes *Māori Scholarship into the 21st Century*, a selection of 21 Manu Ao Academy seminars – chosen from nearly a hundred – on an array of topics relating to identity and self-determination, environment, te reo Māori, education, social and economic issues, and governance and leadership; *Spirit of Māori Leadership*, an historical overview of Māori leadership, covering the academic and leadership experiences of former or current senior Māori scholars; and a collection of inspirational Monday Motivators – *Tihei Mauriora* – available as a desktop flipchart for Māori academics.

The time for new Māori academic leadership is now. One can only be pleased to see the messages of hope conveyed in the chapters that follow. In this book you will learn what young Māori academic leaders have to say about leadership for the future. The next generation of leaders is already in our midst. Our future is in their hands. It is time to pass the baton.

Dr Selwyn Katene
Ngāti Toa, Ngāti Tūwharetoa, Ngāruahine, Ngāti Tama
Director, Manu Ao Academy

Introduction

Established in 2008, the Manu Ao Academy's primary focus was to develop and uplift Māori academic leadership and scholarship. In 2010 Manu Ao established a leadership programme that included a three-part leadership wānanga series and leadership workshops. The three key objectives of the academy were:
1. Accelerating Māori leadership;
2. Strengthening the links between Māori academics and Māori professionals;
3. Advancing Māori scholarship.

As many have argued, Māoridom needs many kinds of leaders who consistently demonstrate integrity, respect, trust, loyalty and inclusiveness. The contributors to the book each discuss the multitude of ways leadership manifests itself in academia and, although each author has worked individually on their respective contributions, a number of common themes emerge that help to define what Māori leadership in the academia looks like and what it needs to prosper. A key theme to be found throughout the book is the dual expectations Māori academics face from both the academy and whānau/hapū/iwi. Another common theme is the mindset of leading to benefit the collective rather than the individual – numerous accounts are given of how to manage the dichotomy of working as an individual in an institution, while trying to achieve a collective vision. While many of the authors discuss personal and hence individual journeys, all seek transformation for the collective. Furthermore, Māori academics provide one of the avenues by which the creative potential of Māori communities may be realised.

When the idea of a book was first posited during the Manu Ao workshops, the new and emerging Māori academics who attended were strongly in favour of writing about our experiences in academia. Many were uneasy, though, about considering ourselves as future Māori academic leaders and writing in the context of leadership. This was simply because, from a Māori world view, the term 'leadership' embraces a number of attributes that are more to do with the well-being of the wider collective, rather than the advancement of our own individual ambitions. Above all, leaders do not proclaim their leadership – a leader is defined in terms of their followers; leaders provide people with clarity, direction and a sense of empowerment. In essence, effective leadership is not so much about seeking to become a leader, but rather about seeing what needs to be done and doing it to the best of our ability. The various chapters within this book have attempted to highlight a number of perspectives on what constitutes new and emerging Māori academic leadership, and the need to continue to develop Māori leaders in academia for the future.

In Chapter One, Nathan Matthews posits that making space within the academy is a necessary and vital component of Māori academic work. In his view Māori academic leadership needs to be founded on a Māori world view and based on Māori cultural concepts that are enacted through tikanga (ways of knowing and doing). In one example he proposes that, given the scarcity of Māori academics, we need to whakawhanaunga – build positive relationships. A Māori academic, as opposed to an academic who happens to be Māori, employs an approach grounded in Māori cultural values, beliefs and principles. An exploration of the dual, sometimes competing, expectations Māori academics face from both the academy and iwi and community is undertaken.

In Chapter Two, James Ataria, Melanie Mark-Shadbolt and Simon Lambert ask the question 'What is Māori Leadership?'. They employ a case study approach and individually discuss past, present and future Māori leaders in order to identify some key leadership attributes and the importance of context in forging good leaders. They each unpack the idea that leadership potential is both an innate and experiential quality whereby good leadership is borne out of the needs of followers – needs that are a manifestation of a specific contextual (temporal and spatial) setting.

In Chapter Three, Meegan Hall provides a personal and inspirational account of the only full-time Māori academic developer in a tertiary institution. She discusses how she turned a trying personal experience into a reflective exercise that crystallised her expectations of Māori academic leadership. Meegan's role requires her to articulate a Māori approach to university-based academic development and leadership that promotes Māori academic success in ways that are both culturally and professionally appropriate. Through her endeavours she has determined four key principles that underpin Māori academic realities: tuakiri (identity), pūkengatanga (skills), tikanga (practice) and whanaungatanga (relationships). Meegan identifies the challenge as finding a balance between those sometimes competing goals that affect our tuakiri, our identity as Māori academics. Given this context, it follows that Māori academic leaders need to create and maintain the space for their staff to be Māori as well as academics and to do both well, with integrity and credibility.

In Chapter Four, Heather Gifford and Amohia Boulton consider Māori academic leadership from within an iwi development context. According to the authors, iwi are realising that academics can be a valuable asset. In their research they discovered that the qualities prized most highly are the ability to think critically and strategically; the ability to analyse and make sense of vast quantities of data quickly; and the ability to present complex information to iwi in a way that allows iwi to make informed and robust decisions. Contrary to the qualities required of Māori academics who remain within the academy, where good Māori leadership is founded on a Māori world view and enacted through tikanga, academics who work with and in iwi are not necessarily expected to have an intimate knowledge of iwi tikanga, tribal lore or whakapapa. Heather and Amohia also suggest that if new and emerging academics are to develop into a leadership role, in and for iwi, they will likely require skills and qualities not necessarily learned within a tertiary education setting – such as notions of reciprocity and leading through service.

In Chapter Five, Marewa Glover explores the idea that leaders are vested with the power to define, protect, decide and develop. She considers Moana Jackson's 'specifics of power' from an academic and research-based perspective. Marewa posits that research is about uncovering what is really going on, removing the rose-tinted glasses of the bright-sided and contributing strategically to comprehensive solutions. Māori academic leadership needs to strive to make room for every child and every woman to succeed. Marewa refers to Foucault's 'regime of truth' and asserts that as leaders we need to first understand notions of power within ourselves and how we exercise it.

In Chapter Six, Mel Cheung invokes powerful imagery of metamorphosis and transformation to explore three key concepts in Māori academic leadership. She discusses the role tika (truth), pono (justice) and aroha (love) have played in her personal transformation and how they ensure she stays passionate, focused and grounded on her journey. Mel also stresses the immense importance that mentors have played and continue to play in her transformation in academia.

In Chapter Seven, Paul Whitinui looks to the past for ideas about what constitutes effective leadership and how those ideas might better inform how we lead in Māori teacher education contexts today. He considers the historical leadership attributes proposed by Te Rangikāheke of Te Arawa and Himiona Tikitū of Ngāti Awa and how these attributes are still relevant today in our various disciplines as Māori academic leaders. The eight different talents – 'Ngā Pūmanawa e Waru' – that chiefs were expected to acquire are considered in an academic and contemporary context. Paul adapts these talents by considering five whakataukī, important to the understanding of how to lead, as distinct from notions of leadership. This is further developed by conceptualising four culturally inclusive attributes to help ground our roles as Māori academic leaders working with/in the academy.

In Chapter Eight, Phillipa Pehi and Reremoana Theodore share a vision for the future of Māori academic leadership based on the idea of interconnectedness and values associated with working together – mahitahi. They link interconnectedness with the principles of collective leadership and draw on their own experiences, particularly focusing on the sharing of, collective participation in, and contribution to, the processes and acts of leadership. Furthermore, they articulate the concept of leading together via notions of responsibility – having responsibility, taking responsibility, sharing responsibility and being responsible.

In Chapter Nine, Margaret Forster posits that kaitiakitanga is a form of environmental leadership that can achieve the three goals of Māori development proposed by Professor Sir Mason Durie: to live as Māori; to actively participate as citizens of the world; and to enjoy good health and a high standard of living. She presents the case of a community driven to achieve kaitiakitanga, underpinned by mātauranga and informed by whakatauākī. Margaret's example of kaitiakitanga as environmental leadership from her own tūrangawaewae demonstrates that while leadership manifests in many ways, relationships and actions are fundamental to achieving hapū environmental rights and interests

In Chapter Ten, Katarina Gray-Sharp delves into the origins of the academy and academic institutions, and juxtaposes that history against principles of Māori leadership developed over generations. She pares back the layers to reveal what form leadership might take, considers the space in which the principles might operate and proceeds to reflectively apply a principle to the space. The discussion is offered as a means of describing the negotiation between a Māori identity (in the form of a pātere), academic acculturation (an essay with citations) and an ever-present alterity (reflection).

In Chapter Eleven, Piki Diamond paints a narrative of challenges overcome, of possibilities dreamed, of potential realised. She shares her journey through and to academia, and lessons she learned along the way. At odds with how the system was assessing her understanding of and engagement with 'visual arts', Piki realised it stemmed from cultural differences based on gallery-valued dogma and the conceptual knowledge formed within the mainstream paradigm. Not discouraged in the least, Piki, showing her creativity, determined to change the system from within – in so doing demonstrating leadership.

In Chapter Twelve, Dan Hikuroa considers Māori academic leadership from the perspective of a scientist. He proposes that a principal responsibility of scientists is to communicate the knowledge they generate to the nation that supports them. He further posits that scientists should consider society more in their research – from determining what questions should be asked and involving communities in the process of generating knowledge, through to ensuring transfer of the knowledge generated. Dan then discusses what Māori academic leadership entails and concludes by focusing on Māori academic leadership in the sciences.

In Chapter Thirteen, Renei Ngawati delves into the reality of the dual responsibilities of Māori academics – one borne out of job descriptions and the other out of whakapapa. She presents a discussion based upon the thesis that Māori leadership within academia today is still about negotiating a path where our obligations to, and aspirations for, Māori are realised. Further, Renei posits that while Māori staff development initiatives do exist in academic institutions, the capacity afforded to enabling academic teaching staff to grow Māori success is not always clearly visible, or indeed accessible.

Māoridom today requires leaders in academia who can communicate effectively, foster inclusion, engage others, create a collective vision, set aside personal agendas, promote the strengths of individuals and, most importantly, appreciate and respect the differences people bring to the table. Each chapter provides a comprehensive view of the experiences, challenges and issues facing many new and emerging Māori academic leaders in their respective roles. In contrast, many Māori academic leaders possess a number of attributes and qualities that enable them to operate in academia with poise, confidence and in good faith. A common theme highlighted throughout the book is that, for many Māori academics, these sorts of skills often go unnoticed, or fall under the radar of what many, including themselves, define as quality forms of leadership. Factors attributed to service were more prevalent in evidencing effective leadership in academia. No doubt, the perspectives of those who contributed to this book will be eagerly sought in preparing the next generation of Māori academic leaders.

Paul Whitinui, Marewa Glover and Dan Hikuroa

CHAPTER **1**

He Toka Tūmoana:
Māori leadership within the academy

Nathan Matthews

Introduction

Leadership is a topic that is often discussed and debated. Māori leadership, in its various guises, is not immune to this as attempts are made to define and categorise the features or attributes of a good leader and good leadership practice. Just as it was traditionally, leadership continues to be important to the welfare and well-being of Māori in contemporary society as described in the following whakataukī (proverb) from Ngā Puhi:

> *He toka tūmoana he ākinga nā ngā tai.*
>
> *A standing rock in the sea, lashed by the tides.*
>
> *(Kawharu, 2008)*

This whakataukī describes the role of a leader in traditional Māori society as an important buffer between their people and external pressures and issues. It also illustrates the position of Māori leaders within the academy who have to mitigate and balance a range of cultural, professional and personal pressures from both within and outside of their institution.

This chapter will examine a range of issues associated with Māori leadership within the academy. First, the situation of Māori knowledge and understandings within the Western academy will be described. This will be followed by an examination of the importance of Māori cultural concepts as a foundation for Māori academic leadership. How do these concepts impact on the understanding of leadership and its practice within the academy? It will also explore the idea of community in relation to the role of Māori academics within Māori society, particularly through the idea of utu (reciprocity) and how this impacts on research and career choices. Finally, the reflections and experiences of the author, an early-career Māori academic, will be described in regard to scholarship and career development.

Māori knowledge within the academy

The inclusion of Māori knowledge and scholarship within the Western academy has been one of contest and conflict. Māori have contested the space within the academy as they have sought to have Māori knowledge legitimised and validated. When we considering the status of Māori knowledge within the academy, and as an extension Māori academics, there has often been an uncomfortable fit. This is due to the fundamentally different way in which knowledge is viewed. Māori knowledge derived from a Māori world view considers knowledge and the world in a very different way than the conventional Western academy. As Smith (1992) explains, 'New Zealand universities are part of the wider international community of Western knowledge but in the New Zealand context are still grounded strongly in the colonisation process' (p. 4). She goes on to write: 'Education was a primary vehicle for the assimilation and colonisation of Māori and the university system continues to elaborate this system further through the specialisation of knowledges and the development of groups and hierarchies of intellectuals' (Smith, 1992, p. 6).

The Western academy with a focus on disciplinary knowledge boundaries is counter to the Māori holistic understanding of knowledge and the world. Its very structure serves to continue unequal power relations within the academy through the marginalisation of Māori knowledge. Therefore, a primary role of Māori academics is to work to break down discipline boundaries through the provision of moral leadership that questions these dominant social relations and structures (Smith, 1992, pp. 7–8). This imperative is reflected internationally in Native and Indigenous Studies, where Indigenous academics face the same power paradigm and ongoing contest for space. Mihesuah (2004) writes that while most scholars

> are concerned about their jobs, promotion, profit and power ... the major difference between the camps is that Native and non-Native scholars fighting the status quo are concerned about the welfare of tribes, empowerment for Indigenous peoples, inclusive stories of the past and present, and overturning the colonial structure ... (p. 33)

The main themes then are the attempts to find ways to create space within the academy and to create conditions whereby Māori academics can maintain their links with communities. This is a 'dual edged accountability' that Māori academics have to their university and communities (Pohatu, 1998, p. 329). Durie (1995) also notes this duality and contends that it is a unique challenge that Māori academics face and that maintaining the balance between these obligations creates further pressure not felt by most non-Māori academics.

Within the contest for space that Māori have been engaged in since the time of Sir Apirana Ngata in the early and mid-twentieth century was the development of Māori Studies as an academic discipline within the New Zealand university system. This was not without controversy and contest in itself and occurred between the late 1940s and 1980s as the various universities developed and established departments and schools.[1] This has provided a space within the academy for Māori knowledge to be preeminent and at the centre of the approach to teaching, learning and research. Māori Studies departments are still subject to the structures and policies of the institution that serve to promote the interests of conventional knowledge systems and thus still have a limited autonomy. Elsewhere within the institutions, progress at varying levels has occurred with the acceptance of Māori knowledge within the conventional Western disciplines. However, beyond Māori Studies, Māori knowledge often remains in the margins. Indeed, other disciplines have used the existence of Māori Studies as an excuse to pick and choose, i.e. ignore, whether Māori knowledge is acknowledged within their practice.

As noted, this creation of a space for Māori knowledge within the Western academy has been an ongoing contest. It has been waged on an ideological plane around ideas of marginalisation and validity of knowledge, and it has been waged on a more structural level in terms of the establishment of Māori Studies. Māori Studies is now embedded within tertiary institutional structures throughout New Zealand. However, the status of Māori knowledge within those institutions continues to require persistence and proactivity to ensure that it remains and extends beyond its current position and situation.

Māori leadership

Leadership has always been important in Māori society and various writers have attempted to describe and define the characteristics that contribute to a traditional Māori understanding of leadership. Two notable accounts of Māori leadership from the nineteenth century are those of Tikitū, of Ngāti Awa, and Te Rangikāheke, of Ngāti Rangiwewehi. Both described the qualities that were desirable in a leader. These qualities related to the specific needs of Māori at that time; they were directly associated with the context in which Māori were living (Grove, 1985). Te Rangikāheke identified eight main principles to describe effective Māori leadership. These were: bravery; war speeches; food procurement; feasts of celebration; restraining the departure of visiting parties; council speeches; welcoming guests; and looking after visitors (Hōhepa

& Robinson, 2008). Tikitū also identified eight principles: knowledge of, and industry in, obtaining food; ability to mediate and settle disputes; courage in war; ability as a strategist and leader in war; knowledge of the arts of carving; knowledge of how to look after people; knowledge of how to build large houses and canoes; and a sound knowledge of tribal land boundaries (Hōhepa & Robinson, 2008). There are commonalities between the principles identified by both men; however, the context of their respective environments is reflected in their principles. Te Rangikāheke, prior to the land wars, had a focus on the hosting of guests and various types of speechmaking, while Tikitū, following the land wars, had a focus on military activity, food production and maintenance of tribal land. As in these examples, leadership in contemporary Māori society is dynamic and the contexts varied.

Within modern academia the subject of leadership is also important. Issues such as the development of Māori academic leadership and succession planning for current Māori leaders are continuing considerations. The Manu Ao Academy was established in 2008 to develop Māori academic leadership and Māori scholarship. In 2010, Manu Ao instituted a leadership programme that included a three-part leadership wānanga series and leadership workshops. The various speakers came from an array of leadership roles such as judges, academics, politicians, business people and corporate tribal leaders. They each presented their own ideas of contemporary Māori leadership drawn from their own personal experiences. One of the recurring themes in the various presentations was the importance of Māori cultural concepts in informing the leadership practice of many of the presenters. The way in which these concepts were described differed between speakers, but the centrality of the Māori world view articulated through the application of the cultural concepts was constant. Associate Professor Manuka Henare, Justice Joe Williams and Professor Te Ahukaramu Charles Royal each presented sessions that shared a commonality in that their approaches were all founded upon a Māori world view based on cultural concepts.

Both Henare and Williams asserted the importance of various cultural concepts in informing their leadership practice. Despite the difference in their professional positions, they both posited this idea as fundamental to their own leadership approaches. They believed that it was this world view that differentiated Māori, and Māori leaders, from others. The range of concepts that might be used to define and describe this world view might vary slightly from one person to another, but fundamentally Māori concepts such as mana (status), tapu (protected, sacred), manaakitanga (hospitality, kindness), tikanga (custom, rule) and aroha (love, concern) are the foundation for Māori academic leadership (Henare, 2010; Williams, 2010). Henare also intimated that one of the issues for a Māori leader was that they were still expected to participate and support their own community, tribal or other, development. This was different to his non-Māori colleagues, who were able to focus primarily on their own interests and careers. For Māori academic leaders who adhere to a Māori world view this was not the case, as tribal and community obligations remained important (Henare, 2010).

Royal had a similar focus when he spoke of aroha (love, concern) as a foundational concept upon which his actions and beliefs are based. He also posited the idea that effective leadership is based on incremental quality development. He described this development using the concept of 'Iti nei, iti nei', which he defined as small quality steps. Therefore his template for effective leadership was one based on a Māori world view that focused on deliberate quality development rather than a rushed or ad hoc approach (Royal, 2010).

The importance of the Māori world view is also highlighted by Penetito (2011), who asserts that:

> The world is considered value-bound (aroha, manaakitanga). We learn those values from the social world (whanaungatanga/kinship, tangihanga). We internalise them and they become part of us (whakapapa, reo). They cannot be set aside (mana/power and authority, tapu/sacred and prohibited). We come to know the social world as being essentially relativist and where multiple realities are the norm. Everyone has his/her own story to tell and variation is the reality (tikanga). (p. 83)

This world view and the cultural concepts that make it up are fundamental to how we each behave and relate to others and the world around us. The understanding of tikanga is also important in academic leadership. In the third wānanga, Te Ripowai Higgins (2010) stated that the ability to enact and understand tikanga was a fundamental skill required in modern leadership. This understanding means that a leader can adapt tikanga and its application to suit modern situations and relationships. In contrast, she used the term 'tikangakore' for those who have no understanding of tikanga. Higgins used examples from Te Herenga Waka Marae at Victoria University that showed that the way in which tikanga is enacted on the marae in a university setting is flexible and pragmatic but that ultimately 'correct' tikanga must be acknowledged and adhered to. She also promoted this as an important characteristic for personal behaviour and as the way in which Māori should approach their roles within academia and their scholarship. Her perceptions and examples supported the ideas raised earlier by Royal, Henare and Williams.

In a Manu Ao leadership workshop at Massey University, Professor Roger Maaka described Māori intellectual leadership as being founded on solid scholarship and administration. He asserted that Māori academic leadership was about creating and maintaining space within the academy and fostering the development of young Māori academics. In these points Maaka was alluding to the internal pressures that are associated with being Māori and working within academia. He saw a difference for those in Māori academic leadership positions, as opposed to non-Māori, in the role of continuing to advocate and strengthen the status of Māori knowledge and Māori scholars within New Zealand universities. He specifically considered the need for effective succession planning to ensure the continued development of Māori scholars within the academy and to allow for the support of current senior Māori academics who often have to fulfil a multitude of roles due to a lack of Māori academic capacity within the universities. Another significant point he made was the assertion that the application of cultural concepts and tikanga that inform the way in which Māori view the world is the difference between Māori and others within an academic context (Maaka, 2010).

Overall, the consensus from these sources is that Māori leadership, academic or otherwise, must be grounded in a Māori cultural world view. How this is specifically articulated may differ from person to person, yet the fundamental importance of Māori cultural concepts and practices remains. After all, without the presence of these features, what would be the difference from any other form or style of leadership?

Māori leadership within the academy

A defining characteristic of Māori leadership, as described earlier, is an approach that is based on a Māori world view. Therefore as Smith (1992, p. 7) states, 'Māori academics are part of and yet separate from the traditional intellectual tradition'. While trained in the methods and approaches of the Western academy, because of the Māori world view and Māori culture-based approach to the world and knowledge, Māori academics have different priorities and responsibilities to non-Māori academics.

Senior Māori academics, as with their non-Māori colleagues, are called upon to lead their various academic units, schools, departments and centres. The paucity of capacity, as noted earlier in the chapter, creates a situation that is different from that of most non-Māori academics, in that Māori academics often have to hold these administrative and academic leadership roles for long periods of time. With few Māori at senior levels, they not only have little option but to assume these roles, but also have fewer colleagues with similar experience and seniority to provide support and relief. It also increases the demand for academic and professional mentoring of Māori academics who are new to their positions and often still completing postgraduate qualifications.

Key aspects of Māori academic leadership should include a 'moral leadership in the questioning of dominant social relations' and a commitment to engender change (Smith, 1992, p. 7). To be a Māori academic leader is not to be passive but to be proactive in your own endeavours and in your support of others. This is a demanding requirement as it reflects the ongoing responsibility of Māori academics to ensure that their institution values and validates Māori knowledge and research – the contest for space.

An important dynamic in the role of Māori academics is the link and responsibility to the community. Smith (1992) locates community at the heart of leadership, stating that:

> *Within Māori society the leadership role of Māori academics is not dependent on our academic status but on our participation within our own whānau, hapū and iwi. Our connections both to the institutions in which we work and to the groups to which we belong place us at an intersection of social relations. (p. 16)*

A Māori academic does not operate in isolation from the community to which they belong. In addition to the traditional kinship structures mentioned by Smith, this can include a variety of 'communities' depending on geographical location, religious belief and personal preference. This link to the community, also noted by Durie (1995) and Pohatu (1998), can be potentially detrimental to a Māori academic's career in regard to promotion, as it draws attention away from the types of research and publishing valued by the academy. Furthermore, this link to local communities does not match the institutional focus on links to international communities (Smith, 1992, p. 9), although this last point has perhaps been alleviated by the rise of Indigenous Studies and, indeed, may have helped drive the development of this new discipline.

Overall, Māori leaders within the academy must fulfil the basic requirements of their academic position, as well as having the additional responsibility of being a critic and conscience of the institution, supporting the development of other Māori academics, and providing research and leadership that is relevant to their communities.

Personal reflections

For an early-career Māori academic there are numerous pressures and challenges involved with working within the academy. These tie directly to many of the issues raised earlier in the chapter, in regard to the status of Māori knowledge in the academy and the roles and responsibilities of Māori academic leaders. In this section I will explore some of these challenges drawn from my personal experiences as an early career academic in two different New Zealand universities, within two different disciplines, Māori Studies and Education.

An important feature of Māori academia in my experience has been the lack of a critical mass. The development of Māori scholarship and the creation of Māori scholars have been a focus of many institutions and organisations for a number of years. Despite this, in the two institutions in which I have worked there has been a paucity of Māori academic staff, with very few at the senior level, and they have mainly, perhaps for obvious reasons, been situated in and around Māori Studies. This has meant that as a Māori academic one is often exposed to higher-level administration responsibilities at an earlier stage than your non-Māori colleagues. It also means that you are frequently called upon to provide the 'Māori perspective' on committees and in areas concerning research development. Although this provides the opportunity to participate in a host of cultural activities that might not be available to non-Māori academics, it also provides further pressure, in terms of time and workload management. As a result, the increasing administration load can have a negative impact on one's research time and outputs. Another feature of being Māori within the academy is the responsibility for leading and supporting Māori cultural practice, such as pōwhiri and mihi whakatau. This could be seen as a double-edged sword: the incorporation of Māori cultural practice into the university environment is something that reflects a Treaty of Waitangi relationship – commonly referred to as biculturalism – but it often falls to the Māori academics to perform this function by default because many in the university are unable to perform this task.

The lack of a critical mass of Māori academics is apparent. Despite, the increasing number of qualified Māori graduates being confirmed at the doctoral level, this in my experience does not translate to an increase in Māori academic staff in higher education. There is obviously a range of issues related to academic staffing levels, but if the institution is only ever prepared to meet the basic requirement that comes with workload formulas and equivalent full-time student funding regimes, then the development of a critical mass will continue to be problematic. Creating more space for Māori to enter the academy requires a major shift in how institutions value our culture, language and ways of knowing and doing.

Personal blueprint

From my experience and research, the following ideas not only help to foster a successful academic career, but can also help the development of a Māori academic leader.

Given the low levels of Māori working within most institutions, it is imperative for an early-career Māori academic to thinks about developing links and networks within and beyond your own institution, commonly referred to as whakawhanaungatanga (the act of building positive relationships). This may occur naturally within a discipline, through research and teaching interactions; however, it is important to use Māori colleagues across your institution as support, and to some degree look past traditional disciplinary boundaries and limitations. Active participation in national networks such as Ngā Pae o te Māramatanga, the Māori Association of Social Scientists, the Māori Historians' Association and the Manu Ao Academy can provide further mentoring and support. They also provide the opportunity to develop meaningful personal and professional relationships that transcend institutional boundaries.

The idea of networking should also extend to those non-Māori colleagues who have a genuine concern and respect for Māori knowledge and our position within the academy as scholars. These critical friends can act in lieu of or in addition to other Māori academics. While these people may never fully grasp a Māori perspective, they can still provide vital guidance and insight in terms of developing a career and navigating the institution. It is important within the university sector to carefully consider what activities and roles will help further your career. You need to develop a clear career trajectory that includes research and teaching in an approach that embodies Royal's earlier concept of 'Iti nei, iti nei'. The importance of research as a criterion for employment and promotion is ever increasing. As Māori academics we need to approach this strategically so that we are continuing to meet the research needs of our communities but are also researching and publishing in such a way that we receive the credit needed within institutions to advance our careers. This career development should not be seen just in personal terms, but also as a way of advancing Māori knowledge within the academy by being in a position to develop and support other Māori academics and further the aspirations of Māori more generally.

Finally, if you are to be a Māori academic, as opposed to an academic who happens to be Māori, I believe that your approach and practice must be grounded in Māori cultural values. As described previously, these values guide our actions and thinking: they are the foundation upon which we can operate within the academy in a culturally appropriate manner. Without this foundation the very essence of what we are doing, and for whom, is questionable.

Conclusion

This chapter has briefly explored some ideas relating to contemporary Māori academic leadership. Specifically, it has focused on a group of presenters who intimately tie their leadership practice and philosophy to a Māori way of understanding the world. They believe that 'good' Māori academic leadership is founded on a Māori world view, built on Māori cultural concepts and enacted through tikanga. Similarly, Māori in senior academic positions who are obliged to assume leadership roles have the external expectations from their own iwi and communities to continue to participate in tribal and community affairs, while enduring the internal institutional pressures that come with continuing to develop the spaces for Māori knowledge to co-exist within the academy. Smith (1992) posits that:

> Making space within institutional structures is a necessary part of Māori academic work. This space has to be made within the very sites of struggle in which we are located. Therefore we are engaged in making space through struggles over power, over what counts as knowledge and intellectual pursuit, over what is taught and how it is taught, over what is researched and how it is researched and how research results are disseminated. (p. 17)

A Māori academic leader within the academy is therefore 'he toka tūmoana', a standing rock that is lashed by tides.

REFERENCES

Durie, A. (1995). 'Kia hiwa rā: Challenges for Māori academics in changing times.' *He Pūkenga Kōrero 1*(1), 1–9.

Grove, R.N. (1985). 'Te Whatanui: Traditional Māori leader.' MA thesis, Victoria University of Wellington, Wellington, New Zealand.

Henare, M. (2010, 16 April). 'Māori academic leadership.' Presentation to Manu Ao Leadership Academy, Waipapa Marae, University of Auckland, Auckland, New Zealand.

Higgins, Te R. (2010, 2 September). 'Māori academic leadership.' Presentation to Manu Ao Leadership Academy, Te Herenga Waka Marae, Victoria University of Wellington, Wellington, New Zealand.

Hōhepa, M. & Robinson, V. (2008). 'Māori and educational leadership: Tū rangatira.' *AlterNative: An International Journal of Indigenous Peoples, 4*(2), 20–38.

Kawharu, M. (2008). *Tāhuhu Kōrero: The sayings of Taitokerau.* Auckland, New Zealand: Auckland University Press.

Maaka, R. (2010). 'Academic Leadership.' Manu Ao Academy, Te Pūtahi-a-Toi, Massey University, Palmerston North, New Zealand. Retrieved from: www.manu-ao.ac.nz

Mihesuah, D.A. & Wilson, A.C. (eds) (2004). *Indigenising the Academy.* Lincoln, NE: University of Nebraska Press.

Penetito, W. (2011). *What's Māori about Māori education?* Wellington, New Zealand: Victoria University Press.

Pohatu, G.H. (1998). 'The University, Māori Studies and Treaty Praxis.' PhD thesis, University of Otago, Dunedin, New Zealand.

Reilly, M.P.J. (2011). 'The beginnings of Māori Studies within New Zealand universities.' *He Pūkenga Kōrero: A Journal of Māori Studies 10*(2), 4–9.

Royal, Te A.C. (2010, 16 April). 'Māori Academic Leadership.' Presentation to Manu Ao Leadership Academy Wānanga, Waipapa Marae, University of Auckland, Auckland, New Zealand.

Smith, L.T. (1992). 'Ko tāku ko tā te Māori: The dilemma of a Māori academic.' In Smith, G.H. & Hōhepa, M.K. (eds), *Creating Space in Institutional Settings for Māori*, Monograph no. 15, Research Unit for Māori Education. Auckland, New Zealand: University of Auckland.

Williams, J. (2010, 15 April). 'Māori Leadership.' Presentation to Manu Ao Leadership Academy Wānanga, Waipapa Marae, University of Auckland, Auckland, New Zealand.

CHAPTER 2

A Commentary on the Changing Landscape of Māori Leadership: Historical, contemporary and future perspectives

James Ataria, Melanie Mark-Shadbolt and Simon Lambert

Introduction

Māori leadership has been sung about, immortalised in prose and debated on many marae throughout the years. In comparison, Māori academic leadership is a much more recent phenomenon that was the focus of a series of wānanga staged throughout the country by Manu Ao, a national inter-university Māori academy, with the support of Ngā Pae o te Māramatanga. These wānanga attracted Māori academics at different stages in their careers from a range of different tertiary education institutions and backgrounds. Literature on leadership and guest presentations by contemporary Māori leaders (academic and non-academic) provided the basis for in-depth discussion and debate on Māori academic leadership. This article was written by three participants in these wānanga in response to the question, 'What is Māori Leadership?'. The authors use a case study approach and individually discuss past, present and future Māori leaders to describe leadership attributes and the importance of context in forging good leaders.

Worldwide, the subject of leadership has been the focus of numerous studies and intellectual discussions (Bass, 1990). Similarly, Māori leadership has also been the subject of considerable analysis and research (Mahuika, 1992; Walker, 1993; Mead, 1994; Whaiti, 1994; Thomas, 2001; Diamond, 2003; Mead, 2003; Pfeifer & Love, 2004; Pfeifer, 2006; Holmes, 2007; Katene, 2010). From a traditional perspective the leadership attributes of Te Rangikāheke of Te Arawa and Himiona Tikitū of Ngāti Awa, as detailed by Grove (1985) and Best (1898) respectively, provide an insight into the attributes and qualities that were required of leadership in that era. Traditional leadership attributes are also eloquently captured in whakataukī and whakatauākī, pepeha (see Mead &

Grove, 2001), eulogies and historical accounts of significant Māori ancestors. These have immortalised the exploits and characteristics of great Māori leaders while providing the following generations with a valuable record of historical Māori leadership. More recently the merit of contemporary Māori leadership has been analysed in reaction to Māori socio-economic statistics and growing opportunities for advancing Māori development and well-being. From the 'renaissance' in Māori culture in the 1970s to the continued expansion of the so-called Māori economy, the space for leadership by Māori as individuals has also expanded rapidly.

In response to this increasing need for Māori leadership, the Manu Ao Academy was established as a national inter-university Māori institution to address leadership issues in academia. A series of leadership wānanga was held in 2010 for emerging Māori academic and professional leaders from tertiary institutions from around Aotearoa me Te Waipounamu. Participants listened to perspectives on Māori leadership from a range of contemporary tribal, political, corporate, social and environmental leaders, and discussed and debated leadership attributes and the complex and diverse range of issues facing Māori leadership today and into the future.

This chapter explores Māori leadership from the perspective of three participants of the leadership wānanga who have used a case-based approach in an attempt to capture their perspectives on historical, contemporary and future Māori leadership. They each discuss the notion that leadership potential is both an innate and experiential quality but that good leadership is borne out of the needs of followers – needs that are a manifestation of a specific contextual (temporal and spatial) setting. Interspersed in their respective discourses will be a range of attributes and characteristics that they believe constitute excellent leadership and that are truly timeless.

He tipua he tangata: Historical Māori leadership – Tā Apirana Ngata

James Ataria

E tipu, e rea, mō ngā rā o tōu ao;
Ko tō ringa ki ngā rākau a te Pākehā
Hei ora mō te tinana
Ko tō ngākau ki ngā taonga a ō tīpuna Māori
Hei tikitiki mō tō māhuna, ā
Ko tō wairua ki tō Atua
Nāna nei ngā mea katoa

Grow up and thrive for the days destined to you
Your hands to the tools of the new settlers
to provide physical sustenance
Your heart to the treasures of your Māori ancestors
as a diadem for your brow
Your soul to your God, the creator of all things

In inscribing this whakatauākī in the autograph book of Rangi Bennett, the mokopuna (grandchild) of Bishop Bennett (Ngāti Whakaue), Tā Apirana Turupa Ngata (Ngāti Porou) gifted a spirit and blueprint that is just as applicable for a well-rounded person as it is for Māori leadership. An analysis of this whakatauākī will be made in relation to the author's views on Māori leadership.

Often referred to by his own people as a 'tipua' (Walker, 2001), or someone with extraordinary talents, Tā Apirana Ngata received an ideal education that would serve his future leadership role well. He was schooled and mentored in the ways of his mātua tīpuna (his father, Paratene Ngata, was a recognised tohunga) and was an outstanding academic in his own right (the first Māori to graduate from a New Zealand university and one of the earliest New Zealanders to attain a double degree in arts and law). He used these teachings as a foundation upon which he embarked on a political quest to address the critical issues of his time, namely alienation of Māori from their land, Māori land tenure reforms and Māori language and culture revitalisation – issues which were to span the length of his political career (1905–43). Tā Apirana Ngata, and his other Māori contemporaries, exhibited strong leadership at a time when pervading attitudes were not entirely sympathetic towards Māori issues – at least politically. His feats, and those of his colleagues, are even more significant considering the harsh political reality of Māori as a political minority in their own country, the social, economic and cultural issues facing Māori, and the prevailing academic and political perspective of the Māori nation as a 'dying race'.[2]

Returning to the whakatauākī, it is obvious that this was gifted to Rangi Bennett as a reminder of the key attributes and values that Tā Apirana Ngata regarded as important in a person's development. However, I contend that the spirit and intent in which this whakatauākī was written, combined with the depth of meaning in the phraseology (Keelan, 2001) and the context of the time that it was penned, have equal significance and relevance to Māori leadership then, today and for the future.

The line 'E tipu, e rea, mō ngā rā o tōu ao' refers to the new beginnings of the plant shoot as it emerges from the seed – a place of energy, of sustenance, of potential, of whakapapa. This also implies that leadership too is predicated on these values and the development of leadership is a continuous and organic process. Of significance here is the emergence of shoots in response to environmental triggers – similar to many examples of Māori leadership that have arisen from a need or specific context. This phenomenon is also eloquently articulated in the whakataukī, 'Hinga atu he tētē kura, ara mai he tētē kura'. However, whether the shoot or tētē kura will grow and mature to reach its full potential will depend much on its environment and the interplay of many different environmental factors – an analogy that I suggest is also true for good leadership.

The lines 'Ko tō ringa ki ngā rākau a te Pākehā / Hei ora mō te tinana' have relevance to this discussion because it encourages a person to look beyond their own culture and comfort zone for skills, experiences and learning that would augment leadership. Attaining these skills will provide sustenance for one's leadership and enhance positive outcomes for those involved with that leadership.

The lines 'Ko tō ngākau ki ngā taonga a ō tīpuna Māori / Hei tikitiki mo tō māhuna' encourage us to wear the treasures of our ancestors proudly as a top-knot for ourselves. In my view this speaks strongly of the traditional Māori values and attributes unique to each whānau, hapū and iwi in this country. The sentiment that is imbued in this particular statement also infers a sense of obligation on Māori leadership that they will remain well versed in the treasures handed down through the ages, like te reo me ōna tikanga katoa, whakapapa, manaaki and whanaungatanga. This statement also suggests that culture is paramount for Māori leadership; while other attributes are important for leadership, they are ancillary to culture. As in the past, these aspects continue to inform and guide Māori leadership and are highly regarded as a key point of difference, an opportunity for innovation and a foundation of strength in an ever-changing country and world.

'Ko tō wairua ki tō Atua / Nāna nei ngā mea katoa' speaks to the importance of spiritual development, irrespective of the particular faith or religion concerned. This phrase could be interpreted as seeking all those things that make one complete or give one a sense of internal and external well-being, particularly the central and foundational role that intangible beliefs and values play in an individual's well-being. In essence this refers to the critical importance of 'knowing thyself', a factor that I consider essential for a good leader. However, it is my view that spirituality, in its broadest sense, is an aspect that is becoming less prominent in leadership by Māori – possibly because of its intangible nature and the fact that it is largely experiential rather than taught.

Reflecting on my professional career, working as an applied scientist in a Crown Research Institute and more recently as a university academic, I consider that Māori leadership in these institutions is viewed by others from a very narrow standpoint – but associated with high expectations. Traditionally, academic and scientific institutions have not provided the necessary support and guidance to first grow the leadership potential of Māori scientists and then nurture that potential. In academia, for example, the often rigid, discipline-focused training and institutional mindset can create a view of Māori leadership that contrasts significantly to community Māori leadership and this can create tensions. In many institutions and science provider organisations it is very pleasing to see that this prevailing attitude is gradually changing: Māori academic leadership is being acknowledged and resourcing is being provided in recognition of the obligations and requirements of Māori academic leadership both in academia and in communities.

In this rapidly changing society, I reaffirm my belief that 'E tipu, e rea' provides a simple but powerful blueprint for Māori leadership that remains just as pertinent today as it was when Tā Apirana Ngata inscribed it in the autograph book of Rangi Bennett.

Contemporary Māori leadership: The Christchurch earthquakes and rising to the challenge
Melanie Mark-Shadbolt

Successful contemporary leadership, regardless of culture or setting, requires three things to be effective: an understanding of followers' needs; playing to leaders' strengths; and surrounding leaders with the right people. In essence a successful contemporary Māori leader is self-aware and a team builder who understands intimately the community they serve. I contend that Sir Mason Durie is a person that possesses these qualities epitomising successful contemporary Māori leadership. However, the seismological events that struck Christchurch in 2012–11 provide a unique example of leadership forged in the heat of a significant natural disaster.

On 4 September 2010 at approximately 4.45 a.m., less than six hours after the final Manu Ao leadership wānanga, people in Wellington were woken by the gentle swaying of their homes, apartments, workplaces and hotels. However, Wellingtonians were soon to discover that what was a gentle rock in the capital was in fact a significant earthquake in Ōtautahi (Christchurch). News reports were quick to come in highlighting the devastation in the Canterbury region and Manu Ao participants from Canterbury were desperate to head home. By 6 a.m. they had decided to forgo previous arrangements, pack and make their way to the airport – driven by an overwhelming desire to get home as soon as possible. Predictably, the airport was full to overflowing with people desperate to get to Christchurch and we were quickly informed that the Christchurch airport was closed for safety reasons (the runway had sustained damage) and that flights into the city would be unlikely to resume until the following day. Additionally, flights to other South Island cities were full to capacity.

The link between this story and successful contemporary Māori leadership, however, begins the night before when Sir Mason Durie asked me light-heartedly, 'So, do you feel like a leader now?' My response was, 'No, actually I don't. I know I'm a great manager and right now I'm happy with that.' However, the events of 4 September highlighted to me that leadership truly is about service and about being willing to make a call when no one else will; that good management is also a key attribute of a good leader, contrary to much thought; and that the context of a situation is a potent catalyst for the emergence of leadership.

As more news filtered through, a bigger picture of the sheer size of the quake began to form. For those of us stranded at Wellington Airport, our nerves were on edge as many of us were unable to make further contact with family and loved ones. Desperate to get home, we were very aware of the situation our families were in and knew that many of them were without power and water, and potentially in damaged homes. While people deal with stressful situations in different ways, the defeatist attitude, or a sense of apathy or indolence that can affect some in situations such as this, is stifling. The response from our group at being stuck at the airport unable to get home was on the whole no different. There were a couple, though, who were able to quickly identify the needs of the group and make decisions that met those needs and inspired the rest of the group to follow – key tasks for aspiring leaders (Rath & Conchie, 2009). Unhappy with waiting around in a crowded airport, they made the decision to keep moving and to look for alternative transport. Within 30 minutes the entire group was in a taxi heading to the ferry terminal, rental vehicles were booked and the majority of the group was home by 6 p.m. that day, having enjoyed some team bonding during the impromptu road trip. A number of things stand out from this event:

1. The inability of the majority to make decisions, especially snap decisions that may adversely affect their peers (action & vision). In this case only two were able to make a decision that would affect the whole group (strength).
2. The willingness of people to step up and take on tasks once the hard decision has been made (teamwork & having the right people). In this situation, once the decision to ferry and drive had been made, people freely volunteered to take on the various tasks involved such as driving and paying for tickets.

3. The manner in which the right decision made for the whole is reflected in the mood of the whole (followers' needs). In this case, once we knew how we were getting home a calmness fell over the group and we were able to focus on the needs of our whānau back in Christchurch.

From my perspective, the sequence of events confirms that the successful leadership factors espoused by Gallup International (Rath & Conchie, 2009, pp. 2–3) are applicable to contemporary Māori leaders, in that successful leaders need to:

1. know their strengths – in this case managing and organising people, decision-making and keeping calm in extremely stressful situations.
2. surround themselves with a good team of the right people – in this situation the leader needed to make the hard decision, but once it had been made, followers stepped up and completed the necessary tasks.
3. understand the needs of their followers and act accordingly – in this case the need was to get home and to keep busy.

It is often in situations like this that one's leadership qualities are given room to shine. The emphasis here is on qualities because it is an individual's qualities that attract followers to want to engage, to be led and inspired by them.

Gallup International interviewed 10,000 followers to ask them what it was they looked for in a leader. The four basic needs the followers overwhelmingly noted were: trust, compassion, stability and hope (Rath & Conchie, 2009). Hope plays a critical role in leadership. Napoleon said, 'Leaders are dealers in hope' and Peter Senge (2010) stated that:

Leadership exists when people are no longer victims of their circumstances but participate in creating new circumstances. Leadership is about creating a domain in which human beings continually deepen their understanding of reality and become more capable of participating in the unfolding of the world. Ultimately leadership is about creating new realities.

We can see people creating new realities and inspiring hope at all levels and areas of society. We see it in action at a global level in successful peace talks and Indigenous collaborations. We see it at a national level when politicians have the courage to plan and advocate long term for a better society, such as in the planning of Whānau Ora. At the community level we look for hope and see it reflected in our response to the earthquake and in the reconstruction of a new Christchurch. We also look for hope as a quality in the contemporary Māori leaders we ask to lead the institutions in which we work.

The message for these leaders then is that leadership is not about power, position and authority. It is about who they are as individuals and about leading by example. It is about their ability to work in relationship with others, about their desire to seek the best for others and about growing teams not individuals. It is also about integrity and the consistency between professed beliefs, values and actions, it is about living and demonstrating those values they espouse in their documents. It requires compassion, love and courage, and it produces stability and trust.

Successful contemporary Māori leaders are proactively working to mobilise people to take positive action. They represent a diverse array of communities and are all around us – we just need to open our eyes a bit wider and look in slightly different places. As Sir Mason Durie said, 'the guy who says he's the leader often isn't', but 'the one quietly doing the work usually is'. Sir Mason Durie is the consummate contemporary Māori leader because he embraces hope and he exudes stability, compassion and trust.

Future Māori leadership: Maui Igorovitch Thung
Simon Lambert

Let me paint a picture of Aotearoa, four generations down the line. The year is 2110, the centenary year of Manu Ao. Tanadium sponsors Tūhoe Trans-Solar Waka Travel (TTSWT) are promoting the event across the Asia-Pacific region to mark their relocation to Beijing and listing on the Hang Seng III Stock Exchange. Aotearoa/New Zealand's population (the name of the country was formally changed in 2019 through the machinations of the now defunct Māori Party) has stabilised at 14 million, and the planet is experiencing the mid-range of climate change predictions first made in the late twentieth century, a level of change which has resulted in mass migration from small islands such as Rangiātea and the Bahamas, and low-lying areas such as Washdyke and coastal Bangladesh. Localised but often intense and violent wars for resources have erupted with monotonous regularity over the past century across all seven continents (although perversely the Palestinians and Israelis have finally found peace). Political-economic trends established at the fall of the Berlin Wall in 1989 have cemented China as the most powerful economy, India second, Brazil third, the US fourth and about to be overtaken by Russia. Aotearoa/New Zealand – a republic since 2023 – briefly joined Australia as the seventh state (as the Australian constitution allowed), then took the opt-out clause at the messy conclusion of the Victoria/New South Wales civil war of 2039. But that's another story.

Manu Ao Inc. accepts only one applicant from each of the three surviving Aotearoa universities (Auckland, Lincoln and Otago), with the remaining applicants coming from among the 38 wānanga, three of which have been Australian Federation institutions since 2037, and the top-ranked overseas institutions hosting Māori scholars (in 2110 these were the universities of Trieste and Kyoto, and the Sao Paolo Institute of Technology).

The keynote speaker for the centennial conference, Maui Igorovitch Thung, was courted by the Asian arm of TTSWT. A Tūhoe robotics irrigation engineer based in Ulan Bator, Mongolia, Maui was seen as an ideal speaker as TTSWT wanted to maximise their Asian market exposure, and he is an urbane polymath, speaking excellent English as well as Mandarin, Cantonese, Thai, passable Spanish and better-than-average Waitaha (which he'd learnt online).

He arrived alone, and was welcomed on the impressive Lincoln marae with its two-storey Ōamaru whitestone and regrowth-kahikatea wharenui. He deferred all speaking roles to a transgender auntie on his father's side, drank only lukewarm green tea and artesian water during the daylight hours, and ate sparingly (a little fish, no red meat). At various times he could be observed admiring clear glasses of the ice-cold, artesian Canterbury water. (All irrigation engineers knew of the Canterbury Plains Water Revitalisation Project of 2018–23, a ubiquitous but still inspiring undergraduate case study.) Then on the final night of the wānanga, when he was asked to speak, he stood, said his mihi, recited that part of his whakapapa that justified his presence and said, 'I know everything about me but nothing about what you want to know. Please ask me so we can all be satisfied.' He then sat cross-legged and waited for questions.

The audience, bolstered by several local politicians and corporate players, was stunned into silence. Presentations were traditionally multimedia, downloaded as hologrammatic packages for distribution and on-sales: 'It pays the rent', as the Ngāti Moki CFO reminded the academics. So many were keen to hear from the Indigenous engineer who joined the final 250 kilometres of irrigation network between China and Iran that Taumutu, TTSWT and Lincoln were certain to make a commercial splash! But Maui sat in mute, Buddha-like reflection, one hand resting on the merino mat.

A small girl, clearly suffering the effects of the solar radiation endured by the poorest in any country, summoned all her courage and spoke in a clear voice: 'Tell us about your ancestors'. Maui Igorovitch Thung began, 'My father, who taught me nine-tenths of what I know about water, which was one-tenth of what he knew, was a third generation Mozzie …' The audience laughed – the term was hardly heard nowadays, being somewhat un-PC from the perspective of over two million tribal affiliates who aggressively pushed their Ngāti Kangaru tribalism. '... And he worked the last surviving mine in Australia, a seam of opals which I'm sure you've heard about.' The audience had, of course, as this seam was under the heritage Sydney Opera House, which was subsequently dismantled and sold to a Russian gas company for them to use as their corporate recreation centre. 'He ended up watering 150,000 square kilometres of Inner Mongolia and enabled the return of 23 million Indigenous people to their tribal homelands, with enough grass for 9 million horses, the latest GE strains of their archaic breeds. Understand,' and here he smiled to the audience and himself, 'my Mongol grandfather is very proud'.

One of the Manu Ao students asked him what personal attributes and characteristics he thought enabled effective leadership. Maui locked eyes on his questioner and recited: 'Courage, openness, ability, excellence. To be a coward is to fail those who, down the ages, braved their lives to bear you. To be closed is to risk ignorance, which leads to misplaced arrogance, the pretence of aping the skills and abilities that the people need without extra horses or spare arrows ...' Maui made a point of drawing on his maternal grandfather's culture, as the lands inherited by his mother were the lands on which his father perfected his art of irrigation. 'And as for excellence, well, to be second best is no shame at all, but,' he smiled, 'it isn't leading at all. And that was what you wanted to know.'

Another Manu Ao student asked about any institutional restrictions that affected him during his academic studies. He answered obliquely,

Because my koroua, who I never met, was killed in the Australian Civil War, my father received a veteran's whānau scholarship to attend the University of West Sydney. He found the ethnic politics too distracting. There was a stir in the students and staff of the University of West Sydney, some of whom had based their careers on the revitalisation of ethnic essentialism, drawing on the writings and political movement of iwi fundamentalists who were prominent in the 2020s but who had faded dramatically in the Aotearoa homelands. It was a great joke to Asian-Māori that these so-called Taoists found a home in Parramatta, the post-bellum capital of New South Wales and the one-time residence of St Samuel Marsden.

So my father transferred to the Calcutta Institute of Robotic Technologies, a crossroads melting pot if ever there was one. There he met my mother, who was from Cambodia, and followed her to lands she inherited from her father, in Mongolia. The rest, as they say, is history.

A girl from the local intermediate stood and asked, what, if any, traditional Māori cultural concepts he drew on in his leadership. Maui laughed and said, 'Сайн юмыг улам л сайн болго! Сайн ч бидний багш Саар ч бидний багш. That is Mongolian, my wife's father's tongue, it means – make good, better. Excel-

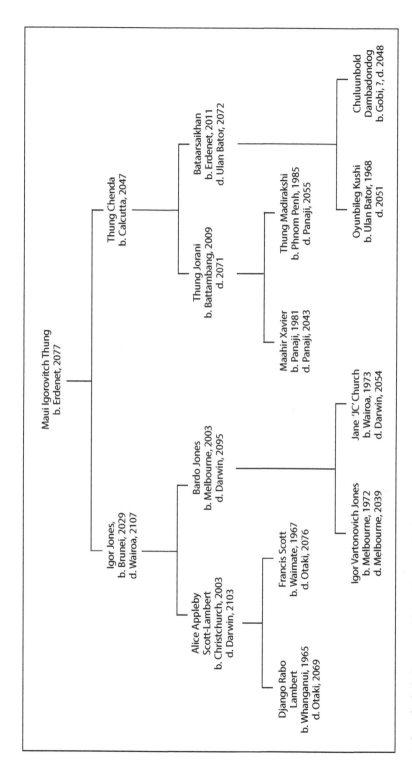

Selected whakakapapa of Maui Igorovitch Thung

Maui Igorovitch Thung
b. Erdenet, 2077

Thung Chenda
b. Calcutta, 2047

Bataarsaikhan
b. Erdenet, 2011
d. Ulan Bator, 2072

Chuluunbold
Dambadondog
b. Gobi, ?, d. 2048

Oyunbileg Kushi
b. Ulan Bator, 1968
d. 2051

Thung Jorani
b. Battambang, 2009
d. 2071

Thung Madirakshi
b. Phnom Penh, 1985
d. Panaji, 2055

Maahir Xavier
b. Panaji, 1981
d. Panaji, 2043

Igor Jones,
b. Brunei, 2029
d. Wairoa, 2107

Bardo Jones
b. Melbourne, 2003
d. Darwin, 2095

Jane 'JC' Church
b. Wairoa, 1973
d. Darwin, 2054

Igor Vartonovitch Jones
b. Melbourne, 1972
d. Melbourne, 2039

Alice Appleby
Scott-Lambert
b. Christchurch, 2003
d. Darwin, 2103

Francis Scott
b. Waimate, 1967
d. Otaki, 2076

Django Rabo
Lambert
b. Whanganui, 1965
d. Otaki, 2069

lence is our teacher. I learnt from those who were better than me at what I wanted to do, what I loved with a passion, and who were doing it in a manner I thought befitting the importance of the task at hand.' This task, as the sponsors and his audience knew, was the bringing of water to the long-dry regions of the world.

An old transsexual farmer then stood and asked, 'What strategies could be employed by contemporary Māori leaders to overcome modern challenges?' Maui thought briefly, then gave another proverb, this time from his mother's tongue, Khmer: '"Riding a buffalo across the mud is easier than trying to swim." I believe an old ancestor of those from the East Coast said the same thing, "E tipu, e rea"? Don't expect to find what you need within your own village, your own 'hood, or especially in such small and isolated countries as Aotearoa. There is no shame in borrowing, only in failing to return the tools.' He paused and ran his eyes across the faces peering at him. 'And the reciprocal favour to those who likewise ask your help.'

His presentation disappointed and delighted in equal measure. Lincoln, trying to leverage a corporate-bond issue with a Chinese company, was disappointed their guest refused to be photographed with the company CEO, a leading fascist politician in north Asia-Pacific. West Sydney was angered by his dismissal of campus iwi politics; Ngāi Tahu were annoyed he did not attend the kapa haka contest in the House of Tahu 2 auditorium, instead going fishing on Waihora (where he hooked seven brown trout averaging four kilos, releasing five and eating two with a group of young people surfing the spit). Tūhoe were simply delighted the keynote speaker was Tūhoe! But the young leaders were almost universally encouraged. This Maui came from what some still called the 'far-aways' – a dismissive term coined in the late 2020s when global climate change was thought to be a regional problem, the last gasp of the deniers. But Maui retained links with all his ancestral lands, and articulated and delivered on a powerful kaitiakitanga discourse through his life philosophy and his work. The pō whakangahau that night entered the realm of the legends often told about Māori gatherings. Otago was delighted Maui Igorovitch Thung anchored their (winning) heritage boat-race team. But that's another story.

Discussion

Māori culture throughout history has endured through collective movements led and inspired by unique individuals, including those discussed here, who draw on the traditional experience focused through the lens of contemporary skills to adapt to and address the issues of the time and particular context. Today Māori society still faces significant cultural, social and economic inequities that are manifested in health, education and crime figures. Arguably, these contemporary issues are as difficult as any other in our history and Māori leadership needs to evolve in order to meet these challenges. This is even more critical moving into the future where local and global contexts and realities are changing at an ever-increasing rate.

However, humanity is being indigenised, as is suggested by the demographic trends here in Aotearoa/New Zealand and socio-political trends nationally and internationally. This is the context and niche that we believe Māori leadership needs to adapt into. To achieve this, in our view, effective leadership will:

1. require constancy of actions that are framed by tikanga (some people do things that work; some people don't) to enable an evolution of individuals, groups, practices and results.
2. be influenced by the fundamental role of scale (individual, whānau, communities, societies, planet) that, in turn, frames the skills, strength and abilities of individuals most suited to lead.
3. necessitate that the focus of any individual is always nested within whānau and the networks that support the whānau – this is now primarily as an employee, emphasising wider economic resilience issues.
4. be cognisant that at the level of the nation state, some groups are more vulnerable than others – in technical terms, they are living in poverty.
5. acknowledge that leadership requires a leader who approaches and can comfortably demonstrate or express the spiritual essence of one's identity.

Māori leadership, whether historical, contemporary or future, is forged in 'te mura o te ahi' – the fires of the issues of the time. Memorable Māori leaders are well grounded in self, understand the needs of others, are passionate about making a difference and are the recipients of good mentorship and counsel – features that we believe are exemplified in the case studies described here.

Acknowledgements

The authors acknowledge the Manu Ao Academy and Ngā Pae o te Māramatanga for establishing and running the leadership forum, and Lincoln University for supporting their participation in the leadership wānanga. We would also like to thank Professor Les Williams of Auckland University for his comments on an earlier draft.

REFERENCES
Bass, B.M. (1990). *Bass and Stogdill's Handbook of Leadership* (3rd edn). New York, NY: Free Press.
Best, E. (1898). 'Omens and superstitious beliefs of the Māori.' *Journal of the Polynesian Society*, 7(28), 233–43.

Diamond, P. (2003). *A Fire in Your Belly: Māori leaders speak*. Wellington, New Zealand: Huia Publishers.

Fowler, L. (1957). 'Māori leaders of the past 1. A new look at Te Kooti.' *Te Ao Hou*, November, *20*, 17–20.

Grove, R.N. (1985). 'Te Whatanui.' Unpublished master's thesis. Victoria University of Wellington, Wellington, New Zealand.

Holmes, J. (2007). 'Humour and the construction of Māori leadership at work.' *Leadership*, *3*(1), 5–27.

Keelan, T.J. (2001). 'E Tipu E Rea: An Indigenous theoretical framework for youth development.' *Development Bulletin*, *56*, 62–65.

King, M. (1997). *Ngā Iwi o te Motu: One thousand years of Māori history*. Auckland, New Zealand: Reed Publishing.

Mahuika, A. (1992). 'Leadership: Inherited and achieved.' In M. King (ed.), *Te Ao Hurihuri: Aspects of Māoritanga* (pp. 86–114). Auckland, New Zealand: Reed Publishing.

Mead, A. (1994). 'Māori Leadership: The waka tradition – the crews were the real heroes.' Paper delivered to the Hui Whakapūmau Māori Development Conference, 10–11 August, Massey University, Palmerston North, New Zealand. Retrieved 7 December 2010 from: http://www.kaupapaMāori.com/assets//MeadA/nga_tikanga_nga_taonga_Māori_leadership.pdf

Mead, H. (2003). *Tikanga Māori: Living by Māori values*. Wellington, New Zealand: Huia Publishers.

Mead, H. & Grove, N. (2001). *Ngā Pēpeha a ngā Tīpuna*. Wellington, New Zealand: Victoria University Press.

Pfeifer, D.L. (2006). 'Leadership: Māori leadership – From good to great.' *New Zealand Management* (4 July). Retrieved 7 December 2010 from: http://findarticles.com/p/articles/mi_qn5305/is_20060704/ai_n24915236/?tag=content;col1

Pfeifer, D. & Love, M. (2004). 'Leadership in Aotearoa New Zealand: A cross-cultural study.' *PRism 2*. Retrieved 7 December 2010 from: http://www.prismjournal.org/fileadmin/Praxis/Files/Journal_Files/Pfeifer_Love.pdf

Rath, T. & Conchie, B. (2009). *Strengths based leadership*. New York, NY: Gallup Press.

Senge, P. (2010). 'Ultimately, leadership is about creating new realities.' Retrieved from: http://onetusk.wordpress.com/2010/10/01/ultimately-leadership-is-about-creating-new-realities-peter-senge

Thomas, D.C. (2001). 'Leadership across cultures: A New Zealand perspective.' In K.W. Parry (ed.), *Leadership in the Antipodes* (pp. 22–45). Wellington, New Zealand: Institute of Policy Studies and the Centre of Leadership.

Walker, R. (1993). *Tradition and change in Māori leadership*. Auckland, New Zealand: Research Unit for Māori Education, University of Auckland.

Walker, R. (2001). *He Tipua: The life and times of Sir Apirana Ngata*. Auckland, New Zealand: Viking Press/Penguin Books.

Whaiti, P. (1994). *Rangatiratanga*. Wellington, New Zealand: Institute for Research and Development in Māori Education.

CHAPTER 3

Principles Over Pinstripes: Developing and leading Māori academics

Meegan Hall

Introduction

As the only full-time Māori academic developer currently working in a New Zealand university, I know from both first-hand experience and the research literature that the development of Māori academic staff has previously been relegated to the 'margins' (Smith, 1992; Irwin, 1997; Asmar, Mercier & Page, 2009; Roa, Beggs, Williams & Moller, 2009). In contrast, the central focus of this chapter is the experiences, identities, aspirations and needs of Māori academic staff working in New Zealand universities today. The ultimate purpose is to articulate a Māori approach to university-based academic development and leadership that promotes Māori academic success in ways that are both professionally and culturally appropriate. It draws on my research about Māori academic development (i.e. the scholarship around the development of academic staff) with a particular focus on how this field can better support Māori academics.

This chapter discusses what motivates Māori people to become academics, how they balance the dual responsibilities associated with working with/in a Māori community and academic institutional expectations, and how they experience being (or reject being) 'othered'. In addition, it shares the issues, pressures and challenges that are routinely faced by Māori academics, and counters these with research findings (alongside my own experiences) about the importance of tuakiri (identity), pūkengatanga (skills), tikanga (practice), and whanaungatanga (relationships) in the process of effective academic development and in the journey towards strong Māori academic leadership (Hall, 2011).

Wearing a suit to work

Many years ago I was working in a part-time, fixed-term academic position while I completed some postgraduate study. One day, I was invited to a meeting with a senior Māori academic manager in my institution. The manager told me that he had heard positive things about me, that he thought I had 'potential' and that he would like to mentor me so that I could move ahead in my academic career. Naturally, I was pleased to receive such positive feedback and was interested in hearing the advice that this manager could give me to help me on my way. So, what was the key tip to get me started? He told me that I should start wearing a suit to work. Other people, he said, would not take me seriously unless I started dressing like a person with authority, and that meant wearing a suit. I have reflected on that conversation many times in the intervening years.

As a young Māori woman, I was horrified to learn that the value of my academic contribution was being measured by some by my ability to wear pinstripes. Was the manager simply reinforcing the beliefs embedded in Tamaterangi's well-known whakataukī, 'He ao te rangi ka uhia, he huruhuru te manu ka tau' (Mead & Grove, 2007, p. 65)? Do clothes really make the person? How does that contribute to academic leadership? On the other hand, I worried that if I did not learn to 'play the game', I would in fact be left on the academic sidelines. What bothered me most, I have come to realise, is that in a so-called intellectual environment I was being told to conform to an outdated and fundamentally shallow view of academic leadership. Yet, as frustrating as that was, it forced me to reflect on my own expectations: What kind of Māori academic leadership did I want to be part of? What kind of leadership did I want for the Māori academic community of the future? What other ways were there to envisage successful Māori academic leaders?

This chapter fuses my own academic career experiences with my research into Māori academic development. As a lecturer in academic development, I work closely with Māori academic staff and have developed a research interest in the ways in which their academic identities and experiences affect their academic development interests and career goals. As a Māori academic myself, this chapter allows me to explore not only what Māori academics have told me about their journeys towards Māori academic leadership but also to reflect on my own journey. Together, these various perspectives help to paint a picture of what it is like to be a Māori academic in a New Zealand university right now, at a time when we are told that funding drivers, research expectations and teaching pressures have never been higher. What are the experiences of Māori academics? How can we engage their energy and potential in ways that enhance their own development, stay true to their own belief systems, and yet are compatible with the university environment in which they are required to operate? In this chapter I explore the role of Māori academic development in the retention and success of Māori academics and the creation of Māori academic leaders.

Experiences of Māori academics

In my research about the experiences that some Māori staff have had in their work as academics, I have become aware of a number of recurring themes, many of which I have also experienced myself. From my experience as a full-time Māori academic developer and from the research literature it is clear that the development of Māori academic staff has previously been relegated to the 'margins' (Smith, 1992; Irwin, 1997; Asmar et al., 2009; Roa et al., 2009). Generic literature about 'one size fits all' academic identities abounds, and even discussion about 'hybrid' academic identities tends to ignore ethnicity as a significant factor. It is within this arena that academic development research and practice is currently occurring.

Unfortunately, it is not only in the academic development literature that Māori academics are invisible. It happens to us within our own institutions, in subtle and not so subtle ways. Take the Māori lecturer who described to me the difficulty of 'being off radar'. While she acknowledged that her sense of being ostracised is 'hardly an unusual story' for Māori academics located in predominantly non-Māori academic units, she admitted to feeling 'a lot of loneliness, a sense of isolation' and to developing a strategy of 'making noise just to make sure that people know you are around'. Another Māori colleague told me of switching disciplines early in her career when she realised that her prior field had 'never really been that interested in different voices'. According to her, 'It's got its eyes fixed firmly on Europe and America for its source of new perspectives. It's not interested in colonial perspectives or Indigenous perspectives.' Another Māori lecturer talked of a lingering sense of racism that excluded him from active involvement in all aspects of university activity. He described how 'there always has been for me at the back of my mind … a feeling that all the other people in the university think that Māori scholars are second rate. And it's deeply, deeply entrenched in the system. It's sort of institutionalised to some extent and you're never going to get rid of it, so I don't care about it mostly but you just know that it's there all the time.' Some Māori colleagues have shared their feelings of inadequacy with me, with one revealing that she felt like she was 'in a continuous cycle of being an imposter … that imposter syndrome' and another describing it as 'this intersection between my

Pākehā learning [and being] Māori' to the extent that she didn't know if she had 'enough "creds" to be considered a good Māori academic or just an academic who tags herself Māori to get free feeds'.

Clearly, to make my point I have not presented a representative sample but, nevertheless, I do believe that the Māori academics that I have quoted here are not alone in their experiences of being marginalised or 'othered' during their academic careers. Indeed, I can add my own experience to the mix – such as the Academic Audit panellist who encouraged me to tell my Māori academic colleagues that they should publish outside of Indigenous journals so that 'we', i.e. Pākehā academics, 'can access their work too'; and the Pākehā colleague in another faculty who remarked to me, on hearing that a Māori colleague had received an 'A' PBRF (Performance-Based Research Fund) rating in the Māori Knowledge and Development category, that 'it's much easier to get an 'A' in that category because they don't have to meet international standards'.

I entered my current academic role with my Māori identity firmly intact and with an expectation that it would be supported and encouraged within that role. For the most part, that has been the case. In my academic development work with my Māori colleagues I regularly find my cultural identity being affirmed and I create and am able to participate in events and opportunities to learn and grow as a Māori woman academic. However, in my wider sphere of activity, when I am doing academic development work that I would describe as being more 'generic' or 'mainstream' I have many times been challenged to defend my world view, my advocacy of teaching pedagogies that I believe are supportive of Māori student achievement, and my advocacy of initiatives likely to increase the number and ability of Māori students. It can be quite lonely and isolated in those moments. While I know I have the full support of my Māori academic colleagues, and many a time I have regaled them afterwards with stories of the racist and uninformed attitudes that I have had to address, I have had to develop strategies to keep myself 'safe' whereby I resort to quoting statistics (like the appalling retention/completion rates for Māori students), and university policies and statutes, and sharing 'carrots' like the increased funding attracted by the higher equity weighting given to Māori postgraduate completions.

Being 'othered' in my own country, in my own university, in my own disciplinary area and even in my own Academic Audit session has been a brutal reality check. I have often wished that I could go back in time and sling some cutting, but professional, retort. Instead, in that moment, while my blood began to boil and I gritted my teeth, I smiled sweetly ... and remained quiet. The question that this notion of being marginalised or othered raises for me in relation to Māori academic leadership is, how can we ensure that, as Te Punga Somerville has lamented, 'we do not participate in our own invisibilisation' (2007, p. 34).

Despite the many challenges, there must be something significant that motivates Māori people to become academics, and my research suggests that it is not the salary or lure of a professorship that drives them to persevere in their academic careers. Every Māori academic that I have spoken to about what motivates them to be academics has given me responses that fall within the following four broad categories: the contribution that they can make to Māori society and culture; the scholarly activity and outputs that the work allows; the influence that their previous life experience has on their pursuit of an academic career; and the enjoyment that they get from academic work.

Māori colleagues have often told me that by working as academics they see themselves as playing an active role in transforming New Zealand society, ideally in ways that improve the lives of Māori people or lead to a better understanding of Māori perspectives, experiences and beliefs. For example, one talked to me about wanting to disseminate her research widely because of an underlying commitment to wanting 'people's views to be more educated and transformed so they really see what Māori people are like'. She felt driven to do research and teach her students in a way that would bring improvements to the life experiences of Māori people in wider New Zealand society.

Another Māori academic explained to me that 'one of the other strong, strong drivers is building Māori capability, building Māori capacity'. Her sense of duty to the Māori community went beyond just herself and her desire to perform well in the role but also extended to other Māori colleagues and students, and her desire to nurture and support them into their own successful academic careers. That sense of wider responsibility led her to take on mentoring roles, and she explained how 'it's looking at who's around you, who you grow, who you can pick up and bring in to grow because there aren't enough of us'. This motivated her in her work to be constantly seeking opportunities to help other Māori scholars and to be 'picking up those people and making sure that things are put in place … that's my ambition and drive …'.

Another Māori lecturer emphasised to me the importance of capturing Māori knowledge and scholarship on paper for future generations. She spoke of creating a legacy and of contributing on a wider scale to Māori society and culture, not only for iwi and hapū but for Māori scholarship generally. Embedded in that notion was the principle of not taking 'the easy road' and her belief that Māori academic work needed to be approached as an opportunity to produce something significant and substantial.

Māori academics have also told me of how their career paths were influenced by their previous life experience, whether it was their undergraduate study experience, their family influence or their prior employment. For example, one told me about how, because of her upbringing, she had chosen to work in an area that supported Māori student achievement. Another told me of needing to be academically successful in order to contribute to a whānau legacy. Another spoke of her realisation that her previous professional career was limited in scope and clashed with her religious beliefs: 'I knew that if I stayed there my trajectory would sort of taper off ... so I thought that being an academic would be more consistent with my faith too.'

A distinctive dimension of the Māori academic experience is the need to balance the expectations of both the Māori community and the academy. While I have found that this balancing act is rarely a source of complaint, it is a dimension of the work that seems distinctive to Māori academics and results in what I've come to refer to as a kind of dual scholarship. For example, one Māori lecturer talked about how 'the work that you do is not really yours and it is actually more of a public thing ... your promotion is not necessarily an individual promotion but it's actually a promotion for the work that you've done, not because it's yours, again, but because it's a Pākehā mark of respect to your Māori work within the faculty'. This linked to her strong sense of duty to perform on behalf of the Māori community and to meet their standards, and also to meet what she believes to be the expectations of the Pākehā academic community too, creating for herself a form of double accountability.

Māori academic development and leadership

Understanding how Māori academics experience the academy is critical to any discussion about both Māori academic development and leadership. It is important for the academic development discourse because without understanding what drives Māori scholars to do what they do, there is little chance of providing them with appropriate, meaningful and effective academic development. Consequently this produces another form of passive 'othering' of Māori academics. In a similar vein, if we want to produce Māori academic leaders who are strong in their Māori, academic and leadership functions, then appropriate training, support and other development opportunities become extremely relevant.

Given that connection, what elements of the Māori academic experience need more attention, in relation to both Māori academic development and leadership? With the insights gained from interviews with a range of Māori academics, I have come to the view that we need to acknowledge the full range of principles that underpin Māori academic realities, both in the process of effective academic development and in the journey towards Māori academic leadership. I have grouped these principles into four key areas: tuakiri (identity), pūkengatanga (skills), tikanga (practice) and whanaungatanga (relationships).

In talking with Māori academics at my own institution, the overarching vision that has emerged is that we want to be Māori academics with integrity. By that I mean that we need to be able to work for and with our Māori communities, we want to be able to maintain our Māori world views, and we want to be able to observe our Māori customs and practices. But at the same time, we want to be good at our jobs. We want to be good scholars, who produce great research, who deliver great teaching, who can act as the critic and conscience of society and who can meet all of the expectations of our academic institution. For example, not only do we have to meet the expectations of the PBRF process but we also have to meet the high expectations set by our tīpuna.

So the challenge is finding a balance between those sometimes competing goals that affect our tuakiri, our identity as Māori academics. Given this context, it follows that Māori academic leaders need to create and maintain the space for their staff to be Māori and be academics and to do both well, with integrity and credibility. Not every Māori academic will need or want to be able to stand as comfortably at the lectern as they do on the paepae, and vice versa. But for those that do, and my research suggests that such a dual function is a goal for many Māori academics, our Māori academic leaders need to pave the way and make it not only possible but desirable. In addition, my research also suggests that Māori staff need to be supported to develop in ways that recognise a broad range of pūkengatanga, including the disciplinary and cultural expertise that we need to develop in order to operate effectively in both the Māori and university worlds. It follows then that strong Māori academic leadership needs to model and support that dual development. Similarly, all of the Māori academics from my research spoke, in different ways, of their commitment to acknowledging tikanga Māori in their professional as well as personal lives. It appears, therefore, that good Māori academic leadership needs to preserve and champion Māori customary practices in the face of any pressures or disdain from the academy.

Finally, I would suggest that an effective Māori academic leader needs to be able to access, mobilise and value the Māori academic sense of community. Unlike other university members, who may feel an affinity to their discipline or institution, for Māori academics there can be a strong sense of whanaungatanga that draws the Māori academic community together, through academic fora and hui, through whakapapa, and through formal and informal group work.

In Māori terms, the importance of the collective is well recognised – working together to achieve our personal and professional goals, maintain our cultural integrity and achieve success in ways that are culturally appropriate to us. All that remains is for that capacity to be nurtured and utilised as effectively as possible by our Māori academic leaders.

So, on reflection, how have things changed since that initial conversation with the Māori manager early in my academic career? I would like to say that there are fewer 'suits' in Māori academic leadership roles in universities in New Zealand, but that would be untrue. However, there does seem to be more space to be Māori – more places to learn about being Māori, more mātauranga Māori being created and disseminated, and more opportunities to forge Māori academic careers. Perhaps the focus of Māori academic leadership has begun to shift from Tamaterangi's original whakataukī to reflect more of its modern adaptation, 'mā te huruhuru te manu ka rere' (Mead & Grove, 2007, p. 286). As the future of Māori in academia becomes less about the 'feathers' that adorn us, it needs to instead focus on developing the 'feathers' of tuakiri, pūkengatanga, tikanga and whanaungatanga that will encourage Māori academics to soar.

REFERENCES

Asmar, C., Mercier, O.R. & Page, S. (2009). '"You do it from your core": Priorities, perceptions and practices of research among Indigenous academics in Australian and New Zealand universities.' In A. Brew & L. Lucas (eds), *Academic Research and Researchers* (pp. 146–60). Maidenhead: McGraw Hill.

Hall, M. (2011). 'Getting real: How Māori academics are making academic development work for them.' Paper presented at the Higher Education on The Edge: HERDSA Annual International Conference, 4–7 July, Gold Coast, Australia.

Irwin, K. (1997). 'Becoming an academic: Contradictions and dilemmas of a Māori feminist.' In S. Middleton & A. Jones (eds), *Women and Education in Aotearoa 2* (pp. 52–67). Auckland, New Zealand: Auckland University Press and Bridget Williams Books.

Mead, H.M. & Grove, N. (2007). *Ngā Pepeha a ngā Tupuna*. Wellington, New Zealand: Victoria University Press.

Roa, T., Beggs, J.R., Williams, J. & Moller, H. (2009). 'New Zealand's Performance Based Research Funding (PBRF) model undermines Māori research.' *Journal of the Royal Society of New Zealand*, 39(4), 233–38.

Smith, G.H. (1992). 'Tāne-nui-a-rangi's legacy: Propping up the sky. Kaupapa Māori as resistance and intervention.' Paper presented at the NZARE/AARE Joint Conference, Deakin University, Melbourne, Australia.

Te Punga Somerville, A. (2007). 'He kōrero e pā ana ki te toa takitini.' *New Zealand Journal of Media Studies*, December, 10(2).

CHAPTER 4

'Capacity and the Cusp': Māori academic leadership in an iwi development setting

Heather Gifford and Amohia Boulton

Introduction

In this chapter we explore Māori academic leadership from the perspective of academic leadership within an iwi development context. In particular, the chapter presents the views of two groups of leaders: iwi leaders and academics who work outside the academy directly for, and on behalf of, iwi. In this chapter we explore their views on the value of academic training and experience, and the contribution academic leadership can make to iwi development.

The authors, Dr Heather Gifford (Te Āti Haunui-a-Pāpārangi, Ngāti Hauiti) and Dr Amohia Boulton (Ngāti Ranginui, Ngāi Te Rangi, Ngāti Pūkenga) are the Director and Associate Director respectively of Whakauae Research for Māori Health and Development (Whakauae), an iwi-based research centre located in Whanganui. Originally established in 2004–05 as a unit of Te Maru o Ruahine Trust, Whakauae's aims were twofold: to develop the research capacity of Ngāti Hauiti and to offer a broad range of Māori-centred research services nationally and internationally. Since its inception, Whakauae has grown from an organisation employing two staff to one which now has six full-time researchers, two administration staff and a range of casual contract researchers. As a tribally mandated research entity under the auspices of Te Rūnanga o Ngāti Hauiti, Whakauae conducts a range of Māori public health research, health promotion evaluation and capacity building, health services and health policy research.

As one of only a handful of iwi-based research centres, led by an academic team with a strong commitment to the values of inquiry, scholarship and academic excellence, Whakauae operates in the unique space between the traditional Western institutions of learning (i.e. the university system) and the desires, needs and expectations of iwi. To work in this space requires specific leadership skills and attributes, which may or may not be fostered or appreciated by the academy. This chapter seeks to elucidate the qualities of leadership that Māori communities and iwi Māori require of new and emerging Māori academics, particularly of those who work directly with and for the benefit of iwi, in the community setting. To achieve this, the authors have analysed and woven together the kōrero from key informant interviews held with iwi-based researchers and iwi leaders to present a set of themes relating to academic leadership in this distinctive research setting.

The chapter is divided into two sections. The first presents the views of five Ngāti Hauiti members who were asked a series of questions regarding iwi-based academic leadership and how this leadership contributes to iwi development objectives. The five iwi members include three males and two females, with ages ranging from 34 to 78. Collectively, these participants have over 80 years' experience in iwi development and currently hold strategic and senior positions in iwi. Informants were purposively selected by the authors because of the important role each plays as a leader or researcher in iwi development initiatives. Informants' responses were thematically analysed and the key themes are presented below. In the second part of the chapter the authors offer their observations and reflections on these themes. An analysis of the leadership qualities that are required of new and emerging Māori academics in order to meet the needs and expectations of iwi in the contemporary context is also presented. The chapter concludes with recommendations for growing and sustaining academic leadership within an iwi context.

Academic leadership: perspectives from iwi

The key informants we approached to inform this chapter were asked a series of open-ended questions regarding the role academics can play in supporting iwi development; the benefit to iwi of having academic capacity; their expectations of Māori academics; and their experience of having access to academics in Hauiti over the last five years. Two iwi members who themselves are academics working for and with iwi were additionally asked to comment on their motivations for choosing to work as researchers within a tribally mandated organisation as opposed to working within a university or Crown Research Institute. An interview pro forma was completed after each interview and key themes identified. The major themes arising from the interviews are presented below.

Capacity: the contribution that academics make

Informants noted a number of ways in which academics can contribute to iwi development aims and aspirations, with two iwi members commenting that academic capacity was particularly important in the early stages of iwi development:

> At an early stage of development it is critical for the preliminary development of the iwi and this level of importance continues through once iwi are re-established. (Key Informant 1)

> It is very necessary, or it has been, for our development. If I look at some of the people that have been involved over the 18 year period, the people that contributed to our development had academic training and qualifications. So we have relied on their contributions to influence what we do both at a strategic level and at an operational level ... they have been quite crucial to where we have got to. (Key Informant 3)

One informant observed that having access to academics 'informed decision-making, made it more robust, and provided us with the capacity to make sound decisions' and in general, having access to academic advice was of great benefit to the tribal leaders:

> It has forced our Rūnanga particularly to stop and think about a lot of the decisions that we are making because we can see that there is a different perspective on many occasions to what we may have had, coming from the research centre. That shows us that there is a different way of looking at it and we should perhaps consider that other option. (Key Informant 2)

In thinking about the usefulness and utility of academics working in an iwi setting, informants observed that academics possessed particular skills that the iwi could draw upon – skills that were developed and honed as a consequence of participating in tertiary, and particularly postgraduate, study. These skills and abilities included a rational and logical approach to problem solving, critical thinking and systematic analysis; the ability to provide relevant advice in a timely manner; the ability to write; and the ability to communicate quite complex ideas in a clear and lucid manner. As one informant noted:

> The skills an academic brings include development of theoretical pathways forward and an ability to look at things from a critical and strategic viewpoint. I don't care what anyone says it's good to have a theoretical model to work on and then make decisions about how you may depart from it later on. (Key Informant 1)

A second informant commented particularly on the analytical skills that academics bring, and the usefulness of these skills to the wider iwi collective, noting:

*It provides our iwi with the people who can research any area or topic of
interest and benefit to the iwi as a whole ... it provides the iwi with capacity
to analyse reports or proposals that may affect the iwi in any way. (Key
Informant 2)*

In addition to their analytical skills, their abilities for problem definition and
problem solving are also highly sought after:

*And the reality is we have some quite highly qualified members, but not only
that, they are not only highly qualified, they have been through processes
and an educational system that allows them to think outside of the square,
enables them to think about processes and methodologies which could be
useful to us, and as we build up our position, we count on that input to
make, to improve our position. (Key Informant 3)*

When considering the actual contribution that academic leadership makes
to iwi development objectives, one informant noted that from their perspective,
they saw academics as being able to provide the iwi 'with capacity to make sound
decisions, on matters that may have either positive or negative outcomes for the
iwi, or the work that the iwi is doing' (Key Informant 2). Another informant
concurred with the view that academics have a strong contribution to make to
iwi development objectives and that, as a consequence, it is the responsibility of
iwi to support members who wish to pursue an academic pathway:

*So over time if there are iwi members who are interested in developing down
an academic pathway we will definitely support them to do that because
we realise there are major contributions that academics can make to our
development. (Key Informant 3)*

The iwi leaders we interviewed provided a number of concrete examples
of the contribution academics had made to iwi development objectives. These
included the development and evaluation of a smoking cessation intervention
which employed hapū workers to lead both the intervention and aspects of
the evaluation; the provision of investment advice by academics with expertise
in economics and investment banking to advance the iwi's overall financial
position; and the creation within the iwi's tribal structure of an environmental
services arm which is able to provide advice on resource consents and more
recently on fisheries allocation:

*One of the big, significant projects that we, as Ngāti Hauiti, went through
was the smoking research, He Arorangi Whakamua. The reality behind
that project was that that could not have happened unless we had some of*

that academic leadership behind it. What I liked about that project was sure, it might have been academically led, but it was really driven by the identified needs of our whānau. And it led to some great developments, like the establishment of Hapū Facilitators, and I think it's brought some benefits not only to us, to Ngāti Hauiti, because we were able to write some academic papers and attend conferences and deliver findings so therefore it would be beneficial to others. (Key Informant 3)

A further concrete example of the contribution academics can make to iwi was provided by a young scientist working in an iwi organisation:

For example, the mitigation from Genesis around the Tongariro Power Scheme. I can help them to spend that money in ways that directly benefits the environment, i.e. how do you do stream planting? How do you do wetland restoration? How do you get your fish back? How do you get your eels back? So that we are not wasting that money and spending it reinventing the wheel and making those mistakes that have been made across the country in terms of ecological restoration. And that means our streams are healthier, our cattle and our stock that our people farm are healthier so they get better profits from their farms and they can supply the marae better, because they can get eels and kōura from their streams for hui ora, hui mate. (Key Informant 4)

Iwi expectations of academics

In order to be of use to the iwi, to help advance iwi development objectives, it is not enough to be a highly qualified academic, or proficient in your field of expertise. Iwi leaders themselves have their own expectations of academics and how they can best work with iwi to advance iwi development goals. The iwi members we spoke to agreed that academics are expected to show leadership; to provide an informed critique; to take a broader strategic view, and be aware of the outside influences that may impact on iwi aspirations; to lead discussion and planning; and where necessary, be sufficiently linked into the iwi structure to call on iwi members to help where required:

We need people, people who are trained to think about what they can do for the iwi, rather than what iwi can do for them … people that will get involved in iwi politics and iwi business. Academic training gives them those qualities that I was talking about before, being able to push aside the rubbish and get to the core of what's important to the iwi. (Key Informant 2)

*I look for those who have degrees of interest with Ngāti Hauiti, not
necessarily with the development but they might just come back to the marae
once or twice and think, 'Oh I might be able to help out here'. So it's those
ones who I normally would follow up. Cos there are ones who have achieved
very, very high in academic circles but they are not involved with marae
or hapū or iwi developments cos they've got other lives. So I am looking
for certain characteristics in a person. Yes, academic achievement, interest
in Ngāti Hauiti, but also the other factor is time, and have they got time
available and if they've got all those, and if a project comes up which matches
their interest then I will marry the project up with them and ask for their
support. And by and large I think all of them have actually helped one way
or another if they have those characteristics. (Key Informant 3)*

Iwi leaders also commented that to be of use in an iwi development
context university-trained academics need to be available and accessible to
the leadership, be known and visible to the wider iwi collective, and have a
long-term commitment to iwi development. The tribal leaders we interviewed
commented that they expect academics to commit to a long-term relationship
with iwi, and that in their experience, this expectation was always met:

*[We expect] a high standard of achievement, we have completion of projects
and we also have developed a strong commitment by those people that have
taken part. Very, very strong. Once in they are in, they are in for the long
haul, not just for one project ... and I think it's the same for anyone that gets
involved but I think if you match it up, if you match projects up with what
they are interested in that just takes it to the next level and they just carry
on, carry on supporting, which is what we are after. (Key Informant 2)*

Academics as iwi members

When asked whether there was a difference between drawing on the skills of any
university-based academic and those who whakapapa to, and work directly for,
iwi in iwi-based organisations and research centres, our informants noted that
there was a clear distinction between the two. The iwi leaders we interviewed
commented on the additional commitment that iwi-based academics bring to
their work and the unique perspectives they offer as academics and as members
of a hapū or iwi. One leader spoke about the lack of objectivity that academics
can bring if they whakapapa to the iwi, as their decision-making and advice
will be informed by the impact such decisions will have on them and their
family and future generations. While in a more Western setting such 'vested
interest' would be viewed negatively, from an iwi development perspective this

same lack of objectivity is regarded as a distinct benefit of receiving advice from academics who are also iwi members:

I am of the view that it is actually advantageous for people who are going to give us advice to be members of the iwi. Probably several reasons behind that, they do have a vested interest. That's a positive thing because it means when they do give rationale, reasons, even decisions, they are making them in the knowledge that this is going to affect them as well as their descendants. So this is an added responsibility that they have, [rather] than just being an out-sourced consultant who basically provides advice and leaves and who has no responsibility for what happens afterwards. (Key Informant 3)

Another iwi leader commented that, ideally, academics needed to be actively involved in iwi development, to enable the iwi collective to access their skills and expertise in a more timely manner:

[We] have people in the iwi, not directly involved in the leadership who we can call upon from time to time, for specific things, but they aren't always available. [We] need people in positions where the iwi can actually use them. Capacity within the iwi is important but also the time and space to react quickly to iwi needs. (Key Informant 2)

It is becoming evident that academic capacity now exists within iwi in a way that it did not previously, and that this academic capacity stretches across various fields and disciplines. In the context of Ngāti Hauiti alone, a relatively small iwi comprising some 1200 members, informants identified postgraduate academic leaders in the fields of health research, economics, law and business, with more junior academic leadership in environmental management and ecology. Furthermore, these iwi leaders see the support of emerging and senior academics as a rapid way of building up the intellectual capacity of the iwi and further enhancing iwi capacity and capability:

You wouldn't necessarily get that [intellectual capacity] in the short term naturally. You could get it in the long term naturally, in other words, sort of evolving development but you are talking about a couple of generations before you get to that level of thinking. But because academics have been through those processes they actually are well ahead of where we might be if we had to wait and quietly evolve those processes. So I think definitely academics play a prominent role in our development otherwise we would have to wait a couple of generations before we could get to where we want to be. (Key Informant 3)

Motivations for working in an iwi context

We asked two iwi-based researchers to explain their motivations for working as academics in iwi settings. By far the overwhelming reason for working in an iwi context is out of a passion and desire to help, assist and support iwi and iwi development objectives, to work for one's peoples and use one's skills for the benefit of the iwi:

> There is the obvious pull towards iwi in that once you have a set of skills in life, whether they be science research skills, or business management or te reo skills, as a Māori there is, I think, a pull and a sense of responsibility and a sense of duty to utilise those skills for the betterment of iwi. So that's a factor. But there's also a factor in that I get to work within my iwi area, so physically I get to stay within my iwi area which wouldn't be a possibility if I was working for a Crown Research Institute. (Key Informant 4)

The opportunity to set the strategic direction, to drive your own research programme, to be autonomous within your work, to make a difference with applied or translational research were also cited as strong motivations for working in an iwi-based research centre or tribal organisation. One informant noted that their current position as a researcher for iwi allowed them to have 'some chunky research projects, some freedom, and some budgets, and some responsibility really' (Key Informant 4). The other informant also viewed working for iwi as an opportunity to be embraced:

> I saw a lot more opportunity for growth, and development, and autonomy and support in Hauiti ... I got a whole chance to develop up a research centre in whatever way I thought was good to develop it. So that was a challenge and something I really embraced I guess. (Key Informant 5)

Being able to investigate areas of direct interest to iwi was also cited as another motivation behind working as an academic outside of the university system. This ability, in conjunction with the trust that is bestowed upon iwi-based researchers and academics, is one of the key differences between working in a more traditional research institution and working in an iwi-based setting:

> Often there is a divide though between Māori academics who often are based in universities and getting that information, [they're] not even disseminating that information. It's just like, cos even when [they're] disseminating, it's like, 'here I am, I am the academic and I am going to tell you this information that I know'. Probably not many iwi have the model that Hauiti has really, and probably not many iwi have scientists working in their environmental units ... I think there is a different relationship; I think there is much more

trust when you work for the iwi, there's much more of a sense that you are researching things that are useful to the iwi, that they have a mandate and a control over, as opposed to, 'you're someone that sits in a university and comes and tells me this'. (Key Informant 4)

However, the other informant noted that in addition to these reasons, the decision to choose to work for one iwi rather than another, where they also had whakapapa connections, was made easier because of the characteristics of the iwi themselves:

There were several things that attracted me, that made it easy to decide to work in this iwi setting. One was that there was an incredible value placed on academic skills and knowledge … it was smaller, it was more accessible, there was a very strong relationship with iwi leaders … and I saw an iwi that was very willing to look at change, look at forward thinking, it was very strategic, I thought, around how they were developing policies and stuff like that. (Key Informant 5)

The cusp: Realising the value of academics in an iwi context

While all the informants agreed that there is value to having access to academic capacity in iwi development, throughout the iwi development lifespan, one informant noted that the realisation that academics can be a valuable asset in iwi development is a relatively recent phenomenon for some iwi members:

We're on the cusp I think of recognising it [the value of academic leadership] more. And it's being forced onto us because we're going through the claims process, and we find we're … in the wilderness if we haven't got that input. (Key Informant 1)

Another informant agreed that at a tribal level, the wider iwi membership has been slower to understand the value of academics to an iwi's long-term goals:

I don't think, for some iwi members, what we do is useful, or accessible or relevant. I've tried to talk to the Rūnanga and talk to some of our iwi members about research ideas … and I guess some of that hasn't been, there hasn't been a huge response to that. (Key Informant 5)

The recent realisation of the value of academics has partially arisen from exposure to research knowledge carried out under the Treaty of Waitangi claims process. One leader talked about a conscious decision they had made to seek academic input and review of material that had been developed by researchers engaged by the Crown as part of the Treaty settlement process. Despite this leader's insistence on seeking academic advice from within the iwi when the iwi is reviewing these documents, other iwi members still questioned the value of seeking this advice from among their own:

Because there is still a total misunderstanding of what an academic is ... 'What do we need them for?' 'What do they know?' You know? And they're probably thinking, 'What do they know about the iwi history?', but of course that is not what their greatest use is for. So there is that great misunderstanding of what input academics could have. (Key Informant 1)

The challenge for iwi leaders is to demystify the role academics can play, create the conditions under which academics can provide robust advice, and utilise academic skills and knowledge in wider areas of development – in particular, to identify the specific knowledge and skills an academic possesses, and then to recognise when and how to best use these skills to further iwi objectives. Iwi members who, as academics, want to become involved in iwi matters but hesitate as they consider themselves lacking in other areas of knowledge such as te reo or tribal history should not be discouraged from pursuing their goals of supporting iwi development. As evidenced in this quote from an iwi leader, academics may have a contribution to make, in spite of a lack of tribal knowledge:

An analysis of the overall structure of the report is where I expect them to comment ... I don't expect them to know which tupuna's wife took off with some other tupuna. (Key Informant 1)

One informant noted that while the iwi leadership themselves may value having access to academic capacity, expertise and leadership at a decision-making level, for the wider collective of iwi members, a degree of suspicionis still evident as to the role of academics, their value to the iwi and the worth of their work:

I think there still exists somewhat of a mistrust of academics on the ground, so I think that constant feeding back of what you're doing or what you have found out is really important. (Key Informant 4)

This is reflected in the comment of an informant who noted that there is still a tendency among the wider iwi membership to undermine or devalue the role that academics have to play in supporting iwi development. The informant noted it is the responsibility of the iwi leadership to provide a safe environment so that academics are able to openly provide their knowledge and expertise, without fear of recrimination:

I expect academics to lead strategic discussions and planning. But of course I'm not expecting the academic to stand up and do that … that comes with an expectation that we are going to allow them to do that. But when the academic has to stand up and go, 'Hey, Aunty is this alright?' and the Aunty goes 'No, sit down', you know? So it's not an expectation on the academic to put themselves in the firing line! (Key Informant 1)

Reflecting on the kōrero: Desirable leadership qualities

What then, are the qualities of leadership that Māori communities and particularly iwi require of new and emerging Māori academics? Contrary to the qualities required of Māori academics who remain in the academy, where good Māori leadership is founded on a Māori world view and enacted through tikanga (Matthews, 2011), iwi-based academics, those who work with and in iwi, are not necessarily expected to have an intimate knowledge of iwi tikanga, tribal lore or whakapapa to work effectively for iwi. Rather, our informants were clear that the qualities they prize most highly, and which they expect academics to possess, are the ability to think critically and strategically; to analyse and make sense of vast quantities of data quickly; and to digest complex information and present it to iwi in a way that allows iwi to make informed and robust decisions. New and emerging Māori academics, if they are to be useful to iwi and iwi leaders, will be expected to have highly developed critical thinking skills; to be able to communicate effectively in a range of forums, including to lay people; and to possess a toolkit of theoretical and conceptual frameworks that can assist iwi to rapidly make sense of highly complex information. In addition, academically trained leaders will be expected to be open to different and competing views, to be disciplined, hard-working, conscientious and available to iwi.

In the course of conducting these interviews we identified a divergence of views between the iwi leaders and the people they represent, as to the value of having academic leaders present in, and working for, iwi. Whereas the iwi leaders we interviewed wholeheartedly support and recognise the value to iwi development that academic training can bring, they also indicated that some iwi members are yet to be convinced of the value of academics to forwarding the long-term goals of the iwi. Academics are still regarded with a level of mistrust and suspicion and are misunderstood by some of the grass-roots supporters of iwi, especially those who are ahi kā and have remained within the rohe.

That the value of academics may not be universally acknowledged by the wider iwi collective has implications for those academically trained iwi members who are wishing to pursue an academic career in an iwi-based organisation. The sense of mistrust that remains among iwi may result in 'turning off' potential academic leaders, or discouraging them from returning home to work for their own people. This in turn raises challenges for any academic who wants to work with and for the iwi. Consequently, to be an effective academic leader in an iwi setting, there is a range of additional qualities that are required, qualities and skills over and above topic-based knowledge or the ability to write well. Such qualities include tenacity, self-motivation and the ability to bounce back from scepticism, criticism or outright hostility. Furthermore, as Wikitera (2011) observed, these qualities of leadership must also be imbued with the notion of reciprocity and of leading through service. These personal attributes may not necessarily be learned in a tertiary education setting; however, they are vital if a new and emerging academic is to develop into a leadership role in and for iwi.

Coordination: Bringing all the parts together

In our view there is a number of elements that need to converge for academic leadership to be valued and utilised in an iwi context. These elements may be further understood and characterised as being internally moderated (i.e. driven by, or the responsibility of, iwi) and externally moderated (i.e. a consequence of personal skills, attributes and training).

The conditions under which academics appear to work well with iwi are where the iwi is willing to acknowledge, accept and value the work of the academic; respect the academic for the skills and training they bring; recognise the desire and commitment the academic has to work for iwi; and have the resources to provide a working environment where the academic is supported to produce those outputs that sustain an academic career path (autonomy, academic leadership, opportunities for student supervision, publication, networking and conference attendance).

In turn, new and emerging academic leaders must be in a position in their academic career where they can work independently in an iwi context; have acquired knowledge that can be directly applied in an iwi context; possess the desire to work with their own iwi and a well-developed sense of the contribution they can make; possess self-confidence that is at the same time restrained by humility; be responsive to the needs of iwi; be visible to the wider iwi collective; and have the time to commit to address issues of importance to iwi in a timely fashion.

We are reaching a stage in our development as a population where more Māori academics are available, across a range of disciplines, to work for iwi than at any previous point in our history. Furthermore, a number of iwi are in positions, post-Treaty settlement, where they could possibly invest in research and development activities. However, few iwi are currently funding and running their own iwi-based research organisations or investing directly in research and development activities without external funding support. As a consequence, for many iwi there is a heavy reliance on voluntary contributions of time and expertise on the part of the academics. What, then, are the varied opportunities available for Māori academics wishing to contribute in an iwi setting?

In our exploration of the topic we consider that there is a continuum of opportunities for leadership, and new and emerging academic leaders must realise that this will not always result in a direct full-time research or teaching role. Contributions by academic leaders can be made by serving on rūnanga; through project-specific work in fields such as economic or environmental development; through appointment to management positions with the iwi; by partnering with iwi in research projects; by negotiating with iwi to 'host' supervised student-led research; and through direct employment as a part-time or full-time researcher.

We believe the time is right for iwi to build on their development objectives by maximising the untapped potential that currently exists among their own iwi members who are academically trained. Some iwi have already begun to realise the potential that lies within this latent resource by hiring academics as contractors and consultants. Others, meanwhile, are starting to realise the value of research in a development context and are looking to develop their own research centres. We, as the trained academics, have valuable skills, knowledge and expertise and by acting in a strategic manner we can synchronise all the opportunities available to move past the cusp and bring together iwi and academics in a way that ensures the academy is alive and well in a tribal development context.

REFERENCES

Matthews, N. (2011). 'Reflecting on Māori academic leadership.' *MAI Review*, 3. Retrieved 8 August 2012 from: www.review.mai.ac.nz/index.php/MR/article/view/457/689

Wikitera, K-A. (2011). 'Travelling, navigating and negotiating: Māori leadership challenges in the 21st Century.' *MAI Review*, 2. Retrieved 8 August 2012 from: www.review.mai.ac.nz/index.php/MR/article/view/439/660

CHAPTER 5

Te Manaaki i ngā Kaiārahi Māori: Looking after Māori leaders

Marewa Glover

Introduction

'To look after' is an old saying meaning 'to take care of'. In this chapter, I do talk about looking after our leaders, but I talk more about how leaders are expected, perhaps integrally to their role as a leader, to look after others in a broader sense. That is, they take care of their constituency. My title is a play on words, in that it can also mean looking after leaders who have gone before. Past actions of leaders have been a trigger for my thinking on Māori leadership presented here.

If 'looking after' is integral to the role of a leader, then leading is what people do when they look after others and it is thus a skill and role that is assumed or imposed and practised from early childhood – for instance, when young children look after their younger siblings or playmates. In order for them to lead, however, the ones being looked after need to agree, acquiesce or submit. In some way they hand over some power. Leaders are thus vested with the power to define, protect, decide and develop – what Moana Jackson (2010) has called the specifics of power:

> *Power to define – that is the power to define the rights, interests and place of individuals and collectives;*
> *Power to protect – that is the power to protect, manaaki and be the kaitiaki for everything and everyone within the polity;*
> *Power to decide – that is the power to make decisions about everything affecting the wellbeing of the people; and*
> *Power to develop – that is the power to change in ways that are consistent with tikanga and conducive to the advancement of the people. (pp. 10–11)*

Jackson's (2010) very clear definition of power, and thus of mana – the generic name given to the concept of power (p. 10) – is prefaced by the acknowledgement that these are human constructs developed for the purpose of looking after land and people. The people being looked after, however, are not always aware of, or conscious of, giving over some of their power. Society often imposes leaders, resulting in others finding themselves an unwilling or unsuspecting follower. Awareness of the distribution of power in relationships is not necessary, however. Many people remain unaware of their place in society, that they are being led, that they are affected in many ways by the decisions and actions of leaders. This was partly the point of the development of a 'philosophy or jurisprudence of law' (Jackson, 2010, p. 5). I propose, however, that leaders at least should be aware of the power vested in them, of the power they have assumed, and of the influence and benefits that flow to them as a result.

This expectation that leaders remain conscious of power and their use of it adds to the already very high expectations placed upon Māori leaders (Smith, 2004). Of Māori leaders, Member of Parliament Tariana Turia has said, 'good leadership must have integrity … We expect them to show integrity and honesty' (Turia, 2001). There is also a very strong dictum against criticising Māori leaders. In the same speech, Tariana contended that:

> … there are always the detractors who are poised and waiting; ready to criticise our Māori leadership. The most severe Māori critics of Māori leadership are themselves identified by the whānau, the hapū and the iwi from which they draw their whakapapa. In criticising an individual, they are also criticising the whānau, the hapū and the iwi from whom that individual draws their leadership rights. So when we criticise, let us take care as to who it is we are criticising, because if the whole is indeed greater than the sum of its parts, then we are also criticising the iwi from which that individual comes.

Thus, it is with some trepidation that I embark on this reflection on Māori leadership. I do not mean for my iwi to be in any way implicated by this, neither do I seek to hold the whānau, hapū or iwi of my exemplars accountable for the actions (or not) of some individual who has given me cause to question. I am thankful to peers who I consulted: they expressed fear for me and warned against referring to any well-publicised cases where Māori leaders have been trashed and mocked by the media, used by members of the colonising dominant culture to further their case against Māori. After all, we cannot know the real story behind such biased and intentional attacks. I have decided, however, that I can reflect on my personal experience of leaders and leadership, which is one of the objectives of this book.

Jackson's 'specifics of power' have been used as a framework for my reflection. I have also mainly drawn from experiences encountered in my career in public health and Māori health policy and research particularly. My primary expertise in Māori smoking, and the devastating consequences of that for us, and my long involvement in tobacco control have provided me with rich and varied contacts and experiences across the whole country.

Power to protect

One day, when I was flicking through the latest news on the *New Zealand Herald* iPad application, with its crystal-clear photos connecting me to the famous and infamous, a Māori story caught my eye – it was illustrated with a photo of a well-known Māori leader. This was a male elder of distinction, head of at least one, if not more than one, important Māori organisation, a status he'd held for as long as I'd known of him. It was uncomfortable for me to see him though, as I have also seen this revered and respected elder in a dressing gown (and he's not my father).

When I was just a newbie to government consultation with Māori, travelling all over the motu, Māori male leaders like this were often contracted to front the expeditions of Government officials, to roll out the brown carpet and get hui happening and Māori people talking. It changes your view somewhat of Māori leaders when people of stature like this come knocking at your hotel door late at night dressed, for and expecting sex. He was old enough to be my father and I saw him just as sick for thinking of me in a sexualised way and approaching me to consummate his fantasies. When I told a mentor, an older Māori woman, that this had happened, she relayed that, in her circles at least, he was known for this.

This example raises two questions for me about Māori leaders: By what actions do leaders undo themselves and earn just demotion? Should not leaders watch out for and protect the young, the vulnerable, the naïve? If my tuākana, older wāhine, Māori colleagues knew of this man's like for wine and girls, what kind of leadership is it to put me at his table and leave me alone to manaaki this guest of honour? I can understand that a person's position and influence, at least as perceived by the audience needing persuasion, could be so useful to the whānau, hapū, iwi or all Māori, that the perceived benefits could be valued more highly than the physical and mental well-being of a few women abused by such men. And that we are still battling for resources and for a higher status for our people (over others) and that war begets casualties. But we are contemporary Māori living in a supposedly ethical and professional world. We espouse ancient values: aroha, manaaki, pono. We claim deep attachment to tikanga, to living according to systems of ethics and 'we expect our leadership to be deeply connected to our own value system, to our own ethics and protocols and to our language' (Smith, 2004, pp. 11–12).

The power to protect is, I propose, a fundamental function of both Māori male and Māori female leadership, one called for by many Māori women leaders before me. For example, 'in the late 1970s, Donna Awatere said that she dreamed of an Aotearoa where it was safe to be born a Māori girl. Where we would have equal opportunity to survive, flourish and enjoy the benefits of being tangata whenua in Aotearoa' (Reid, 1994). Thirty years later Māori girls are still the most vulnerable in our society. Māori girls are more likely to be sexually abused than European girls and girls from other ethnic groups (urban: 30.5 per cent vs 17 per cent; rural: 35.1 per cent vs 20.7 per cent) (Fanslow et al., 2007). Māori children are victims of homicide more than any other ethnic group, and the majority of victims of other family-member homicides were Māori (2.05 per 100,000) (Martin & Pritchard, 2010). Māori women have the highest current smoking prevalence rate (44 per cent) (Ministry of Health, 2012). In 2006, only 45 per cent of Māori babies were exclusively and fully breastfed at three months compared to 60 per cent for 'other' and 55 per cent for 'all ethnicity' babies. Lower breastfeeding rates mean reduced health benefits for these women, their children and their whānau. For many of us Māori women, life has been or still is about surviving, living on despite the sheer force of the often repeated waves of violence (the racism, sexism, the whakamā of running out of food, of having white social workers newly immigrated from Britain run you down, of having teachers campaign against your child).

Royal (2010) has proposed that an essential quality of leadership is aroha, to have a deep love for the world and for people. In his talk to the inaugural Manu Ao leadership course (ibid.) he promoted compassion and forgiveness, and he urged the joyful participation in the sorrows of life. I don't believe it is useful to romanticise humanity – some people are capable of deep evil and to change that we need to remain conscious of it. Some behaviours are not okay and if you have been a victim of those 'sorrows of life', as I have been, you know that those experiences are absolutely not joyful. I doubt I will ever entreat a survivor to forgive the paedophile or rapist that abused her or him. There is no joy, no 'gift' in sexual abuse, or breast cancer or having your pēpi die of SIDS. Aroha, first and foremost, is the absence of abuse. If we could just stave off, or better yet stop, the violence (from parents, teachers, social workers) towards children and the male partner violence towards women (and children), like the leaf that innately turns to the sun, our children and women would similarly be able to grow unfettered towards the realisation of their potential. Māori leadership needs to make that happen, needs to make room for every child, every woman to succeed.

As a researcher, I believe that Māori (and non-Māori) researchers need to assist also, and not be seduced by the priorities of research funding sources, that encourage a focus solely on the 'Quest(ion)' to 'Dis-Cover' (ibid.) something new and previously unknown. Research is also about uncovering what is really going on, removing the rose-tinted glasses of the bright-sided (Ehrenreich, 2010) and contributing strategically to comprehensive solutions.

Power to decide

At the start of my 'quest' against Big Tobacco, I met a knighted Māori leader – a veteran politician who had participated in decision-making on our behalf for many many years. He was medically trained also, which would have added to his credibility and influence, especially on things health. He was also a known pipe smoker: 'Everything in moderation – even smoking' was his advice to me. He failed if he meant to put me off working to reduce Māori smoking – I stayed steadfast, a useful quality if you plan on becoming a leader yourself.

I have since met and lobbied a few more of our Māori politicians and the ones that smoke all seem renitent to the evidence against smoking tobacco – the biggest killer of Māori today (tobacco smoking is the largest preventable cause of illness among Māori and costs the Māori economy over $260 million per annum in tobacco taxes alone) (Apaarangi Tautoko Auahi Kore, 2003). On some occasions, they become as forceful as the tobacco companies in their defence of tobacco. For example, a stuff.co.nz article led off with the following statement: 'National MP Tau Henare is smoking again and has suggested it is OK for pregnant women to do the same.' The article reported that Henare disputed that 'smoke-exposed babies were born compromised and disadvantaged' and he 'objected to suggestions that children from smoking families were more likely to smoke'. 'Then all my kids should smoke, not one of them smokes and I've got five of them,' he said (Chapman, 2012).

In New Zealand during the period 2003–2007, 61.6 per cent of infants (aged 4 to 52 weeks) who died from Sudden Unexpected Deaths in Infancy were Māori (Child and Youth Mortality Review Committee, 2009)! Smoking when pregnant is a definite and proven contributor to this tragic loss. To support smoking when pregnant – to do anything less than say in a very clear and firm way 'let's get you off the smoke' – is to support the death of Māori babies and the unnecessary handicapping of at least half of all Māori children who will live with more colds, flu, glue ear, asthma, learning difficulties, days off school, and days in hospital throughout their childhood (Glover, Kira et al., 2013). It is an abuse of power to be in a leadership position, to be on the podium speaking for an organisation, a political party, a people; to have the media at the ready and to use that privilege, that chance to say something useful, but instead defend or promote one's personal interests.

Leadership is not always about making things happen – sometimes it's about letting things happen. For example, if a leader has some imperfection, some 'weakness' like addiction to smoking – at least be a closet smoker. Don't downplay the damage caused by smoking, don't belittle or fight the actions of those who seek to remove tobacco from our country and, above all, don't promote it.

In another example, I have had three stop-smoking interventions for Māori blocked from being delivered in different regions in the last 12 months. New pūtea for the interventions was secured. Existing funding was not going to be lost. But Māori people in a position of authority, for their own reasons, decided to pass up the opportunity. The smokers in those regions who want access to new and innovative ways to stop smoking, some of whom would have stopped smoking as a result, will never know they missed out.

There's an opportunity cost to everything and someone, leaders usually, has to decide what to fund and what to turn down. However, 'People who decide how to spend health budgets hold the lives or livelihoods of many other people in their hands. They are literally making life-or-death decisions' (Ord, 2012). Ord generously suggests that poor decision-making in public health is typically done out of ignorance. When lives are at stake, particularly Māori lives, Māori leaders need to demand that appropriate expertise is utilised, even if it means recognising one's own limits (not every leader can fight in every battle) and letting someone better suited talk on the topic. In a constrained funding environment with increasing healthcare costs, decision-makers in public health must understand 'opportunity cost' and cost-effectiveness.

Power to develop

Someone once said that I have too much integrity, which I thought was an oxymoron. How can you have too much integrity? I concede, however, that it could be considered human to struggle with integrity. For example, many health workers struggle to 'walk the talk' (Glover, Nosa et al., 2013) – in their jobs they may be expected to promote a smokefree lifestyle, increased physical activity, minimal alcohol intake and good nutrition – behaviours they do not personally institute. When a Māori leader smokes in full public view – sometimes defiantly so – they send a message that smoking is okay. This is because leaders are looked up to, admired, emulated. Benchmarks are set by their behaviour. The young and people with underdeveloped autonomy are particularly vulnerable to the adoption of perceived social norms. The tobacco industry knows this, which is why, when asked if they smoked themselves, one tobacco company executive said 'Are you kidding? We reserve that right for the poor, the young, the black and the stupid' (Herbert, 1993).

Leaders are role models. If Māori leaders want to improve our lot then they need to heed what they portray and thus approve of. To improve Māori health, we need Māori to stop smoking and we need to reverse the obesity epidemic that is washing over society, adding dangerous layers of fat to anyone with a poor diet and who doesn't exercise 30 minutes a day. If we want to stop Māori children from being abused, if we want to protect their potential and prevent youth uptake of cannabis use, then Māori leaders need to stop smoking tobacco and stop smoking dope. They need to cut the fat, pound the pavements and put a stop to violence in their own homes and cars.

Driving to a stop at a set of lights in Auckland one day, my concerned attention was drawn to the angry yelling occurring in the car next to me. When I recognised the esteemed Māori kuia behind the wheel, I felt ashamed. It could only be family – daughters and moko – I thought, that she'd speak to like that. Which is my point: our children, sisters and moko deserve no less than the polite and respectful behaviour we use in public when talking to people we're trying to impress. We should be no less a leader in the full sense of the word in our own homes.

Te tohu o te rangatira, he manaaki

The sign of a chief is generosity

Leaders understand that people grow, despite the ravages of political and social upheaval around them. Leaders see, foresee and gently guide, manipulate and stand back if needed. Leaders recognise that their own contribution is time-limited and that future potential leaders must be identified and encouraged. Late in 2012, the Honourable Tariana Turia created a bit of a stir among some Pākehā colleagues in tobacco control (and bloggers online) at a parliamentary reception she hosted and was to speak at. It was the national Tobacco-free Aotearoa conference. Tariana has been such a champion for Māori health, especially seen in the progress tobacco control has made while she has been in parliament. We were eager to hear her speak and honour her with our applause, but instead Skye Kimura, a young Māori woman who has moved up in tobacco control to hold the position of Health Promotion Advisor (Tobacco Control) at the national office of the Cancer Society, delivered Tariana's speech. Tariana stood right in the front of the audience and listened and applauded. While some people framed this as a failing of duty, from a Māori perspective this was a beautiful example of Māori leadership in action. New leaders will not be developed and come forth if elders do not mentor, involve, create opportunities and eventually stand aside for them. Similarly, learning is not shared if Māori leaders hang on to positions, rolling over their term until the limit of their term is reached.

Power to define

While this aspect comes first in Jackson's list of the specifics of power, I have put this section last as it seemed more like a conclusion to return to. New Zealand is lauded as one of the best countries in the world to raise children (Easton, 2005), but we have not obtained utopia yet. We do not have a fair and just society. Men and women do not receive equitable benefits, nor are the spoils of the community dished out equitably among Pākehā, Māori, Pasifika and Asian peoples resident in New Zealand. It is hard to rise above the hurts of sexist and racist discrimination, but leaders must try. In his talk to the July 2010 Manu Ao leadership course, Tā Tipene O'Regan warned against Māori becoming like a coloniser if we in turn discriminate against new immigrants. Instead, we, Māori leaders, must work to change the exploitative nature of human beings – which is in each of us who benefits from the inequitable distribution of resources that creates vulnerable groups. We have to be 'critical humanists … change individuals for the better and … improve social conditions for all' (Foster, 1986, p. 18).

There are numerous ways that people in power exclude others and thus manipulate outcomes to their own ends. One way in which current recognised leaders do this is by their own defining of a Māori leader. The criteria we set for recognition as a Māori leader and the expectations we set for Māori leaders can include and exclude. In this chapter and throughout this book we have proposed numerous qualities required of Māori leaders and of Māori leadership. Does it matter if a Māori academic is not involved with their hapū at a flax-roots level? What if they don't even know their whakapapa, except that they are Māori? Are the criteria we set just another way of restricting who can benefit from academic achievement and who can benefit from the shortage and therefore need for Māori at a senior academic level? As Katene (2010) has argued, Māoridom needs many kinds of leaders. There are not enough to go around; though the few that there are, get around a lot. But there is a cost personally, in terms of leaders' health and sometimes, sadly, longevity, and those costs carry over to the whānau as well. As followers, are we looking after our leaders when we demand that they carry on another term? Perhaps we need to look at ways to develop and support younger, less 'qualified' people into leadership, which was one of the issues the Manu Ao Academy was looking to address.

Conclusion

The abuse of power inherent in the process of colonisation is a central precedent of the abuse of power in Māori communities today (Jackson, cited in Glover, 1995, p. 147). Via an exercise of power and the use of violence, the colonisers took away the power of whānau, hapū and iwi to nurture, to protect and to preserve – powers which are basic to who Māori are. These powers were replaced by a model of society that the colonisers brought with them and imposed upon Māori people – one that protects property interests. Under that system, women were chattels of men and had no rights of their own. This macro-political system is mirrored at a micro level within homes when men prohibit and remove Māori women's power to preserve, decide and protect.

Sexual harassment, bullying employees, using taxpayers' dollars for personal gain (be it erotic videos watched in one's hotel room, or the purchase of boxer shorts) and outright fraud are not behaviours befitting ethical leaders today. And when Māori leaders behave badly, all Māori suffer. When the media learns of a Māori leader's indiscretion or an unwise payment, they feast on it and readers harbouring racist beliefs that Māori are inferior feel vindicated. Others swaying in their opinion are tipped and Māori as a group suffer the consequences of the consolidation of the Pākehā 'empire' (akin to the 'masculine empire' described in Adams, 2012), which holds within its collective consciousness that Māori fail. Or as Foucault (1998, p. 63) calls it, the 'regime of truth' that pervades society, which is a kind of 'metapower' in our society, supporting Pākehā dominance and Māori submission to the inferior, dependent role.

Of course there are many, and many more emerging, Māori leaders who are focused, self-aware and ethical. The media is less interested in them, however, and their significant positive works. But all our leaders must think before they speak, consider who's watching before they act, and foresee as much as possible how their own words and behaviours can be used against Māori by the media, the opposition, and industry. It is one of the contributors to Māori underachievement that we allow Māori leaders to get away with abuse of the power they have come into. In order to speak against it, in order to put processes in place to look after leaders so they stay honest and accountable, so they remain leaders that truly do look after the land and people, we need first to understand power ourselves and how we exercise it.

REFERENCES

Adams, P. (2012). *Masculine Empire: How men use violence to keep women in line*. Auckland, New Zealand: Dunmore Publishing.

Apaarangi Tautoko Auahi Kore (2003). *National Māori Tobacco Control Strategy 2003 to 2007*. Wellington, New Zealand: Apaarangi Tautoko Auahi Kore.

Chapman, K. (2012, July 27). 'Smokers the "new lepers" – Henare.' Fairfax News NZ. Retrieved from: http://www.stuff.co.nz/national/politics/7349730/Smokers-the-new-lepers-Henare

Child and Youth Mortality Review Committee, Te Rōpū Arotake Auau Mate o te Hunga Tamariki, Taiohi (2009). *Fifth Report to the Minister of Health: Reporting mortality 2002–2008*. Wellington, New Zealand: Child and Youth Mortality Review Committee.

Easton, B. (2005, July 25). 'Is New Zealand the best place in the world to bring up children?' Presentation to the Wellington Workers' Education Association. Retrieved from: http://www.eastonbh.ac.nz/2005/07/is_new_zealand_the_best_place_in_the_world_to_bring_up_children/

Ehrenreich, B. (2010). *Bright-Sided: How positive thinking is undermining America*. New York, NY: Metropolitan Books.

Fanslow, J.L., Robinson, E.M., Crengle, S. & Perese, L. (2007). 'Prevalence of child sexual abuse reported by a cross-sectional sample of New Zealand women.' *Child Abuse & Neglect, 31*(9), 935–45.

Fletcher, M. & Dwyer, M. (2008). *A Fair Go for All Children: Actions to address child poverty in New Zealand*. Wellington, New Zealand: Children's Commissioner and Barnardos.

Foster, W. (1986). *Paradigms and Promises: New approaches to educational administration*. Buffalo, NY: Prometheus Books.

Foucault, M. (1998). *The History of Sexuality: The will to knowledge*. London, UK: Penguin.

Glover, M. (1995). *Te Puna Roimata. Māori Women's Experience of Male Partner Violence: Seven case studies*. Auckland, New Zealand.

Glover, M., Kira, A., Cowie, N., Wong, R., Stephens, J. & Marriner, K. (2013). 'Health consequences of tobacco use for Māori – Cessation essential for reducing inequalities in health.' *New Zealand Medical Journal* (online).

Glover, M., Nosa, V., Gentles, D., Watson, W. &. Paynter, J. (2013). 'Do New Zealand Māori and Pacific "walk the talk" when it comes to stopping smoking? A qualitative study of motivation to quit.' *Journal of Smoking Cessation*.

Herbert, B. (1993, November 28). 'In America: Tobacco dollars.' *New York Times*.

Katene, S., (2010). 'Modelling Māori leadership: What makes for good leadership.' *MAI Review, 2*. Retrieved from: http://www.review.mai.ac.nz/index.php/MR/article/viewFile/334/477

Jackson, M. (2010). 'In the matter of the Treaty of Waitangi Act 1975 and the Claims in Te Paparahi o Te Raki Inquiry.' Brief of Evidence of Moana Jackson to WAI 1040. Retrieved from: http://www.converge.org.nz/pma/mjwai1040.pdf

Martin, J. & Pritchard, R. (2010). *Learning from Tragedy: Homicide within families in New Zealand 2002–2006*. Wellington, New Zealand: Centre for Social Research and Evaluation, Ministry of Social Development.

Ministry of Health (2012). *The Health of New Zealand Adults 2011/12: Key findings of the New Zealand Health Survey*. Wellington, New Zealand: Ministry of Health.

Ord, T. (2012). 'The moral imperative towards cost-effectiveness.' Retrieved from: http://
www.givingwhatwecan.org/about-us/our-research/the-moral-imperative-towards-cost-
effectiveness

Reid, P. (1994). 'Te Ara Ahu Whakamua.' In *Conference Proceedings of the Māori Health Decade Hui*. Wellington, New Zealand: Te Puni Kōkiri.

Royal, Te A.C. (2010, September 2). 'Academic development: from wānanga to the university.' Presented at the Manu Ao Leadership Academy Wānanga, Victoria University of Wellington, Wellington, New Zealand.

Smith, L.T. (2004). 'Activism, leadership and the new challenges for indigenous communities.' Dr Charles Perkins AO Annual Memorial Oration 2004, University of Sydney, Sydney: Australia. Retrieved from: http://ses.library.usyd.edu.au/
bitstream/2123/1666/1/Smith%20Perkins%20Oration%20USyd%20Oct%202004.pdf

Turia, T. (2001, August 6). 'What our people expect of our leaders.' Young Māori Leaders' Conference, Michael Fowler Centre, Wellington, New Zealand. Retrieved from: http://
www.firstfound.org/Vol.%207New_Folder/turia.htm

Turia, T. (2012, July 9). 'Toitū Māori Health Leadership Summit 2012.' Retrieved from:
http://www.beehive.govt.nz/speech/toitu-Māori-health-leadership-summit-2012

CHAPTER 6

Caterpillars to Butterflies: Learning to lead with tika, pono and aroha

Melanie Cheung

Introduction

When I first started thinking about the idea of new and emerging Māori academic leaders, I pictured monarch butterflies emerging from chrysalises, flapping their wings, and looking at the world full of wonder. This led me to thinking about the children's story about the very hungry caterpillar, devouring all that food to prepare for metamorphosis. We can draw on the very hungry caterpillar story as a metaphor for the hunger for knowledge that results in transformation. But how does this transformation occur? How does the caterpillar really know what the best types of food are to eat? How does it learn to attach itself to the underside of a leaf, construct its tiny chrysalis and finally emerge as a beautiful majestic butterfly? Well ... I think they must have mentors, beautiful majestic butterfly mentors.

Likewise, in order for me to begin emerging from my tiny little chrysalis, I too have had beautiful majestic butterfly mentors that fed my hunger for knowledge and facilitated my transformation. They are the best in the world at what they do. Anybody that knows me knows that I value excellence. I have learnt how to do research to the highest level with these brilliant Māori and Indigenous academics: Michael Walker,[3] Linda Tuhiwai Smith,[4] Richard Faull,[5] Karina Walters[6] and Manulani Aluli Meyer.[7] But they are so much more than just great minds. These people have shown me how to lead with heart and soul and spirit. Their leadership is people-centred, honourable, visionary, transformational, humble, real, compassionate, loving, inclusive and humorous. Each of these people, in their own special way, has shown me how to lead with tika, pono and aroha. This chapter will discuss these three central values of leadership: learning to lead with tika, learning to lead with pono and learning to lead with aroha.

Learning to lead with tika

My mentors have shown me the importance of leading with tika. There are many people in this world that could teach me how to be a good scientist, and maybe even a great one. I have been incredibly lucky to have people in my life today that not only teach me to be excellent at what I do, but they teach me to do this with a heart for the people. To me this embodies tika. To lead with tika is to have a heart for the people.

If we consider tika and tikanga, they are about doing the right things in the right way with the right people at the right time for the right reasons. We can apply tika to our research. We can apply it to our teaching. We can apply tika to our relationships in the academy, and we can certainly apply it to leadership. Tika questions, it asks: What are my motivations? Why do I want to lead? What sort of leader will I be? Am I doing this the right way? To lead with tika is to have a deep ethic that motivates and sustains every part of our lives.

When I think about my motivations to teach and to lead, I am reminded of what my dear friend and mentor Mike Walker has taught me about education: that we are in the business of growing people, the most important thing that you can grow. What a privilege that is! Seeds are planted. Then they are watered and fertilised. A little shoot comes up and, with lots of water, nutrients and sunshine, eventually the plant blossoms. There is a whakapapa that describes this process, the blossoming of the universe at the beginning of time. It's a beautiful thing. Watching your students blossom. Seeing the lights go on. People's lives are forever changed. I have seen this transformation in many of my students and I have experienced this myself.

I was that little shoot that was watered and nurtured and encouraged and supported. Now I get to be the gardener. I get to pass on the legacy that my mentors gave to me. That's what motivates me to lead, to teach, to research, to write. To lead with tika is to pass on the legacy we have been given. To lead with tika is to grow people.

You see, when we think about education as the business of growing people, it changes everything. It reminds us of the bigger picture. It reminds us that transformation is the goal: transformation for our students, transformation for their whānau and transformation for their communities. So while excellence and knowledge are important in the academy and in our communities, the bottom line is that it's all about growing people. 'He aha te mea nui o te ao? He tāngata! He tāngata! He tāngata!'[8] Since people are the most important thing in the world, then there is nothing more important than growing people and helping them realise their potential. To lead with tika is to facilitate transformation.

Learning to lead with pono

Embracing pono in academic leadership is not always easy. To be pono is to acknowledge that you don't know everything. At times this can be really uncomfortable, especially when you want to be the leader that has it all together. I have learnt that it is just as important to know what you don't know as it is to know what you do know. There is a whakataukī that teaches us that we must first crawl as caterpillars, before we can fly like beautiful majestic butterflies: 'Ka nōki te anuhe, ka rere te kahukura.' This teaches us that humble origins are the foundation for success. To lead with pono is to be humble.

Pono is about understanding and identifying your limitations. It's having the ability to tell the writing group that you lead, 'I can't write because I am paralysed with fear that I don't have anything worthwhile to say.' Then everyone starts to talk about their fears and their challenges with academic writing. So we grow closer, because we are honest with each other and we share our struggles. We are all afraid. But together we can all be courageous. To lead with pono is to be honest and real.

It is so important to be who you are! 'Kūkū te kererū, ketekete te kākā.'[9] Unless I know who I am, how can I lead a team? How can I draw on the strengths of my team, if I don't even know what mine are? I can't be an effective Māori leader if I am still struggling with my own Māori identity. For the longest time I was resentful about growing up in the middle of nowhere – in Edgecumbe, Matatā and Manawahē. These are blink-and-you-will-miss-it kinds of places. But that is where my bones are. From my time spent with Indigenous people around the world in small towns, on reservations and tiny little islands, I have come to realise that all the best Indigenous places are blink-and-you-will-miss-it places. These are the grassroots places that have heart and soul. To lead with pono is to never forget where you came from.

I grew up in a small town surrounded by my Māori and Pākehā whānau. We spent weekends and school holidays at my grandfather's farm: docking, shearing, bailing hay, feeding out, moving stock, cooking, cleaning, playing and laughing. We didn't spend much time at our marae, but when we did go there we were welcomed with open arms. Everybody in Matatā really loved my grandparents. They were good people and I am lucky to have that legacy. Because I am the teina I would inevitably end up in the kitchen and to be honest, this is still where I feel most at home on our marae. I love that whakataukī: 'Ka tika ā muri, ka tika ā mua.' When everything's alright at the back, everything's alright at the front! Our kaumātua Uncle Tame Minarapa says that all the time. This reminds me that everybody is important and everybody has a role to play.

If the people aren't fed, then there won't be a pōwhiri. If there is no kaikaranga, then there won't be a pōwhiri. If there is no kaikōrero and no singers, then there won't be a pōwhiri. We are interdependent. We need each other. A good leader recognises this and acknowledges the contribution that each person gives. That is the leader that I strive to be. To lead with pono is to recognise that we are interdependent. To lead with pono is to acknowledge the contributions of others.

Now that I am older, I am grateful that I grew up at home in the middle of nowhere, at the centre of the universe. Because I know who I am, I know where I am from and I recognise that not everyone has had that privilege. Although I wasn't raised at the feet of my kaumātua and kuia, I was still raised with strong Māori values: whānau, manaaki, tiaki, tika, pono, aroha, tapu, noa, tikanga, katakata. These values guide me in everything I do.

Learning to lead with aroha

Aroha has many aspects. It can take many forms. For instance, one of the tutors that I trained once told me that he liked having me on his side because if he ever needed anyone sorted out, he knew where to come. At first I was a little offended by his comment, but I have since made peace with this idea. I am reminded that my ancestor Rangitihi was a warrior chief.

'Ko Rangitihi upoko whakahirahira. Ko te upoko i takaia ki te akatea. Ehara mā Te Aitanga-a-Tiki.' When his head was split open on the battlefield it could have all been over. But he got his head bound with the akatea vine, then he fought on and won the battle. That's my tipuna! The first thing that comes to mind about the meaning of this story is Rangitihi's hard-headedness – his perseverance and resilience. So we are reminded that perseverance and resilience are important leadership characteristics. Never give up! To lead with aroha is to overcome adversity and to persevere.

Even though the whakataukī is about Rangitihi's head, his heart is also implicit. If you think about it, it was actually Rangitihi's great passion and love for his people that motivated him to overcome a serious head injury, to go back to the battlefield and to eventually win the battle. Love is and will always be our greatest motivator. I see so many strong Māori leaders that go to great lengths to sort things out and I recognise that they are motivated by love for their people and passion for their kaupapa. This inspires me on so many levels. To lead with aroha is to be passionate about your people and your kaupapa.

It is also through aroha that I have learnt to embrace all people that identify as Māori. I don't get to define what being Māori is. There are people with fair complexions that have Māori hearts. I have been both student and teacher in Māori programmes that have had blonde Māori, ginger Māori and even Chinese Māori (also known as Horientals). Colonisation and urbanisation have meant that not everyone is secure in their cultural identities. We have had some people that knew their whakapapa, culture and language, and some people that didn't. What is interesting is that because we all felt accepted and loved, we all blossomed. We learnt about aroha through experiencing it first-hand. We learnt about whanaungatanga through living and breathing it. To lead with aroha is to accept others, to be inclusive.

My experience was that studying at university helped me to learn more about things Māori, to learn what I knew and what I didn't know. I think taking part in Māori programmes made me feel like I belonged, and at the end of the day that's what we all want. We all want to belong. My kaumātua and kuia in Matatā teach me that everyone that can whakapapa to us belongs with us, at our marae. That is whanaungatanga, which has its roots in aroha. I think the same idea applies to Māori programmes at the university. If you have a Māori whakapapa, then you belong. It's just that some people still have to learn how to belong. They haven't learnt yet that being Māori is not about what they look like. Culture is not biological; it's not determined by your skin colour, your hair colour or your eye colour. It's determined by your whakapapa and the way that you live your life.

In our cosmogony, right at the centre is a whānau: a mum and a dad and a whole lot of kids (Ranginui, Papatūānuku mā).[10] This reminds me that whānau is at the centre of our universe. That's probably why I work best when I am part of a whānau. This holds true at the university too. I really started to enjoy university when I became a part of the Tuākana whānau, along with other staff and students involved in the University of Auckland School of Biological Sciences' Tuākana Programme. That's when I understood that I might just be able to make it through all the lectures and labs. I see now that, in addition to the Tuākana whānau, I have many university whānau throughout the world: my Māori science writing group, the Centre for Brain Research, the Faull and Dragunow laboratory groups, the School of Māori and Pacific Development, the University of Waikato's Pro-Vice-Chancellor Māori Office, the MAI network, the Indigenous Wellness Research Institute and the Nottebohm Laboratory Group. We share our joys and our sorrows, our ups and downs. You can be sure that where there is whānau, there is aroha. And if we think about education being about growing people, then we realise that building strong university whānau is fundamental to that. To lead with aroha is to build strong whānau.

Conclusion

So that leads us back to the image of the new and emerging Māori academic leaders slowly emerging from their chrysalises. Throughout this chapter I have described and discussed many aspects of tika, pono and aroha that I believe are necessary for very hungry little caterpillars to transform into beautiful majestic butterfly leaders. I am certain that having university- and community-based mentors that lead with heart and soul and spirit are a vital part of this process. I know this because my mentors have been hugely influential on the ways that I teach, research, write and lead. I am certain that they will continue to influence my life for many years to come.

On reflection, the key messages in this chapter are actually about transformation: the transformative process of having people that believe in you. The transformative process of doing things in the right way for the right reasons. The transformative process of belonging. The transformative process of embracing who you are. The transformative process of embracing others. The transformative process of coming to know. The transformative processes of learning to lead with tika, pono and aroha.

CHAPTER **7**

Te Ara Tika ki te Rangatiratanga: Embracing Māori academic leadership in today's Māori teacher education world

Paul Whitinui

Introduction

Contemplating 'effective' leadership in the area of Māori teacher education is particularly timely given my recent appointment to the University of Otago College of Education (Te Kura Ākau Taitoka) based in Dunedin, New Zealand. The appointment coincides with the College of Education's commitment to raising the profile of Māori studies in teacher education and to help foster educational partnerships that are bicultural and respectful of the principles inherent within our country's founding document, the Treaty of Waitangi. In 2007 the Dunedin Teachers' College merged with the University of Otago, and since that time, it has undergone a number of professional and strategic developments to increase the visibility of Māori ways of teaching and learning within the College of Education. Perhaps most importantly, achieving 'buy-in' from the wider Ngāi Tahu/Māori community has been considered vital to growing a distinct and vibrant Māori teacher education programme.

In this chapter, I want to draw on some of the leadership ideas posed by Mead, Stevens, Third, Jackson & Pfeifer (2005) in their working paper, 'Māori Leadership in Governance', as a way of making sense of what constitutes effective leadership and how these ideas might better inform my new role. Leadership, more often than not, has been described as the 'presentation by a person of some identifiable vision that people aspire to and their willingness to follow that leader along a socially responsible mutually beneficial pathway, toward that vision' (Parry, 1996, p. 14, cited in Katene, 2010). Graen and Hui (1999), however, argue that the perceptions of what it means to be a global leader are changing. Today, the global leader is evolving more towards a 'transcultural cultural leader', someone who can transcend their childhood acculturations and show respect for increasing diversity of different cultures, identities and communities. This implies that leaders of the future will not only need to be adept in developing cross-cultural relationships that involve mutual trust, respect and collegiality, but will also need to actively problem solve cross-cultural conflicts and at the same time construct new working cultures in various operations within and across an institution (Graen and Hui, 1999). Given the changing nature of our working environments – schools – it is important to reflect these differences in what we expect graduates to attain from the Māori teacher education programme.

Creating spaces that enable Māori academics to lead requires a genuine concern for the day-to-day behaviours of how we communicate with each other in the workplace. Furthermore, the ability of a leader to motivate others to do more than they believe they are capable of achieving relies on mutually respectful relationships and exchanges of human kindness (Parry, 1996). Today literature about leaders appears to view leaders as too bureaucratic (transactional), charismatic/hero-orientated (transformational), or trait-specific (inherited parent-behaviour characteristics), or it promulgates the view that people either possess or don't possess the necessary leadership qualities (Katene 2010). Of particular interest is the dearth of literature on the perceptions and experiences of Māori academic leaders currently working in such settings, and perhaps none more so than in Māori teacher education, where I now reside.

Traditionally, Māori leadership was based on a communal subsistence lifestyle where a number of different social groupings worked for the collective well-being of the tribe. What is distinct about this form of leadership is that individuals had overlapping roles and responsibilities that were inclusive of the collective aspirations of iwi/hapū/whānau. Today, understanding traditional leadership and its application in a modern context is not well known and, in many ways, lies fragmented or displaced within a neo-liberal agenda. No doubt, how individuals choose to lead in academia will vary and depend on one's family upbringing, character, lineage and experience. Whānau leadership, for example, describes this class of leader as being a kaumātua/kuia, or an elder who is often recognised by members of the family as their 'immediate' leader and, as such, takes on a leadership role at an iwi or hapū level on behalf of the whānau (Mead, 1997; Katene, 2010). Keeping in mind these traditions and the traditional practices of our ancestors, I want to offer some personal reflections, insights and learnings in regards to my new role in Māori teacher education that may well be considered helpful for future Māori leaders considering working in academia.

The ability of a Māori chief to establish kinship ties, alliances and build other strategic networks based on whakapapa was considered a key attribute in growing a tribe's cultural capital as well as the tribe's mana territorially. From a Māori world view, leadership in and of itself is an extension of who we are, our identity, and is committed to enhancing the well-being of the wider collective – iwi, hapū and whānau. Exploring leadership in more traditional Māori times may well provide some key attributes or understandings about how to lead more effectively in my new role.

Ngā Pūmanawa e Waru – The eight talents

Himiona Tikitū of Ngāti Awa described eight different talents – 'Ngā Pūmanawa e Waru' – that chiefs, as leaders were expected to acquire (cited in Mead, Stevens, Third, Jackson & Pfeifer, 2005). These included:

He kaha ki te mahi kai – *industrious in obtaining or cultivating food*
He kaha ki te whakahere i ngā raruraru – *able in settling disputes, able to manage and mediate*
He toa – *bravery, courage in war*
He kaha ki te whakahaere i te riri – *good leader in war, good strategist*
He mōhio ki te whakairo – *an expert in the arts, especially wood carving*
He atawhai tangata – *hospitable, generous*
He mōhio ki te hanga whare rimu, waka rānei – *clever at building houses, fortified sites or canoes*
He mōhio ki ngā rohe whenua – *good knowledge of the boundaries of tribal lands. (p. 8)*

The pūmanawa (talents) model is not only important in illustrating how chiefs, as tribal leaders, were expected to manage everyday social, economic and political dealings, but also highlights the moral and ethical obligations of chiefs to maintain the well-being of the tribe. Instinctively, how might we, as potential future Māori leaders, consider these sorts of talents working in Māori teacher education today? The following are some personal anecdotes of working with the talents above to help grow the Māori teacher education programme.

He Whakaaro Rangatiratanga Tuatahi – Leadership Reflection One

He kaha ki te mahi kai – *industrious in obtaining or cultivating food*

Helping to develop and grow a 'whānau of interest' in the area of Māori teacher education is based on the idea that whānau remain central to the educational aspirations of the tribe. This leadership attribute also implies that every working member of the whānau collective is important to helping to develop a comprehensive, quality Māori teacher education programme that benefits students who enrol. Furthermore, cultivating a positive working environment requires a space (or spaces) that increases the visibility and relevance of the courses that underpin the Māori teacher education programme within the College of Education. Part of my role, in this regard, is to create a learning environment that is inclusive, engaging and respectful of the wider Māori community and their whānau. At the forefront of such endeavours is to always ask, what will enable the Māori teacher education programme at the University of Otago to flourish and grow, and how are we meeting the needs of our iwi, and our Māori students and their wider whānau? These sorts of fundamental questions give rise to other developmental questions: for example, how will our graduates, from within the Māori teacher education programme, be better prepared to meet the wider societal and global challenges related to teaching in the twenty-first century?

He Whakaaro Rangatiratanga Tuarua - Leadership Reflection Two

He kaha ki te whakahere i ngā raruraru - able in settling disputes, able to manage and mediate

The everyday leadership of managing, mediating and settling disputes is an important consideration in maintaining the collective unity of a group. This also requires good leaders to listen attentively, communicate respectfully and make decisions that uphold the integrity of all concerned. Cammock (2001) states that:

Leadership is a dance, whereby leaders and followers jointly respond to the rhythm and call for a particular social context, within which leaders draw from deep wells of collective experience and energy to engage followers around transforming visions of change and lead them in the collective creation of compelling futures. (p. 28)

It is therefore, important that leaders work on – and can demonstrate – inclusivity, develop social cohesion and are non-judgemental towards others and their varying levels of ability. Good leaders know how to build on an individual's strengths and are instrumental in supporting them to overcome their weaknesses.

He Whakaaro Rangatiratanga Tuatoru - Leadership Reflection Three

He toa - bravery, courage in war

The courage of leaders is their ability to make the right decisions at the right time and often in the face of challenging circumstances such as, for example, the current university-wide fiscal constraints, declining student numbers and/ or decreasing staffing numbers. This requires academic leaders to be open to innovative and creative ways of addressing problems, looking at diverse and collaborative solutions. Once identified, it is important to develop a strategy based on integrity (honest communication), passion (drive and persistence), courage (front up to problems) and faith (optimistic, positive and resilient) that will engage all staff to want to be part of developing realistic solutions moving forward. Growing the area of Māori teacher education requires one to be focused, disciplined and resilient in meeting the needs of all concerned, and especially the students enrolled in the programme. Resiliency to manage and cope with everyday institutional pressures and expectations placed on Māori academic leaders also requires poise and a willingness to work through challenges with determination and faith. Inevitably, various levels of resistance towards helping to develop and/or grow the potential of Māori studies in teacher education will require leaders who can reconcile the different attitudes, beliefs, behaviours and values people bring and clearly articulate why Māori studies in teacher education is both necessary and beneficial for all student teachers to be aware of.

He Whakaaro Rangatiratanga Tuawhā – Leadership Reflection Four

He kaha ki te whakahaere i te riri – good leader in war, good strategist

The art of generalship is based on the idea that leaders need to be able to lead a community forward and improve its standing by enhancing the collective well-being of the group in all areas of society – socially, economically and politically. This requires the ability of leaders to identify a range of alliances, networks and like-minded people who truly value the purpose of having Māori studies in a teacher education programme within a mainstream tertiary institution.

He Whakaaro Rangatiratanga Tuarima – Leadership Reflection Five

He mōhio ki te whakairo – an expert in the arts, especially wood carving

Becoming a leader or expert in a particular academic area or discipline takes time and a real affinity with one's chosen profession. Conversely, having specific experiences and knowledge about a specific discipline or role does not necessarily mean one is necessarily suited to becoming an effective leader. However, understanding the broader set of skills, talents and attributes an individual brings to an academic role enhances the possibilities to develop leadership pathways in the future.

He Whakaaro Rangatiratanga Tuaono – Leadership Reflection Six

He atawhai tangata – hospitable, generous

One of the core values inherent within the Māori world is manaakitanga – hospitality, generosity of spirit and warm-heartedness. Manaakitanga is also about being present and ensuring people feel safe and comfortable about being around you and knowing that you genuinely care for them. This requires that leaders are kind, considerate and respectful to others, and that they genuinely appreciate people for who they are as human beings first and foremost. A good leader is also someone who can demonstrate these attributes consistently and with proper respect and integrity.

He Whakaaro Rangatiratanga Tuawhitu – Leadership Reflection Seven

He mōhio ki te hanga whare rimu, waka ranei – clever at building houses, fortified sites or canoes

A leader's ability to perform is based on ensuring one has the knowledge and skills to manage and complete both small and large tasks in a timely manner. It also stresses the ability of a leader to rally a workforce together for a common purpose and to keep them engaged and motivated (Mead, Stevens, Third, Jackson & Pfeifer, 2005). To date, most of my time has been spent on getting to know people, processes and procedures. The next part of my journey involves learning more about the history of Dunedin as well as reflecting the people of Ngāi Tahu in karakia, pōwhiri/mihi whakatau, waiata, mōteatea, mihi and whaikōrero.

He Whakaaro Rangatiratanga Tuawaru – Leadership Reflection Eight

He mōhio ki ngā rohe whenua – good knowledge of the boundaries of tribal lands

Living in Ngāi Tahu is both a privilege and an honour. As a significant professional partner working in Māori teacher education, I am responsible for consulting and working closely with Ngāi Tahu, the Office of Māori Development, and Te Tumu School of Māori, Pacific and Indigenous Studies, as well as the wider Māori community, on all matters concerning Māori educational needs and aspirations. The university's strategic plan is clear that working with local Māori in this region includes the three papatipu rūnanga (local tribal collective councils) of Ngāi Tahu within the Dunedin region – Moeraki, Ōtākou and Puketeraki, as well as being inclusive and cognisant of the other 15 papatipu rūnanga within the area of Ngāi Tahu. Understanding the tribal boundaries also coincides with my willingness to continue to develop my understanding about the language (i.e. dialect), traditions, stories and culture of the people of Ngāi Tahu, while working to improve educational outcomes for Māori students in all areas of education. An integral part of the journey includes learning about mātauranga Māori (Māori ways of knowing, thinking and doing) as it relates to Ngāi Tahu tikanga and to develop a Māori teacher education programme that reflects these interrelational, tribal and culturally explicit ways of knowing, thinking and being.

Leadership demands and expectations

Personally, my choice to work in academia was not an iwi/hapū/whānau decision but rather an individual decision brought about by my own experiences in education and the need to look at ways of improving the ongoing underachievement of Māori students. The talents above are not new ideas per se, but they are new to the way I think about my new role as a leader working in Māori teacher education. Having being involved in Māori education for the past 16 years, nothing could have prepared me for the added responsibility and expectation this new role entails. I remain, however, optimistic that my vision of being prepared to make a difference in the area of Māori education, and in particular, for teachers working in Māori education, will allow me to meet the demands and expectations the role warrants.

Māori aspirations in academia

when I was growing up in my home town of Whakatāne in the Eastern Bay of Plenty, my parents believed that finding a job to support my general way of life was fundamental to becoming a socially responsible adult. As I was a rather overzealous and impatient teenager, the idea of pursing a higher education was often discouraged, mainly because as a whānau we did not have the finances to support me attending. In addition, my own schooling and educational experiences did not encourage or inspire me to think about leaving home and going to university. Also, my sporting prowess as a young teenager provided a safe haven to avoid school and was something I was generally good at doing. My desire and passion to improve the educational outcomes for Māori students emerged in my later years due to my own personal experiences in education and this became a key factor in pursuing a career in education. Consequently, new opportunities became readily available the higher I achieved in my studies and as a result teaching became my preferred profession. I also developed an interest in postgraduate studies and life as an academic seemed to follow naturally, although hard work has always underpinned my success in academia.

Māori achieving in the academy

The number of Māori successfully completing their doctorates in Aotearoa/ New Zealand is growing, but of particular interest is the number of Māori with doctorates choosing not to work in academia. There are many reasons for this, including a lack of suitable positions specific to their area of expertise, the attraction of working overseas and the growing desire among our people to return home to work in their own communities. Similarly, there is now a cohort of Māori with doctorates leading their own research-based consulting businesses – although initially challenging, many have expressed a sense of freedom, outside of an institution, to conduct research that is purposeful, relevant and beneficial to their communities. From a personal perspective, the pressure to return home and to work with my iwi is always apparent, but so too is the drive to make a difference in institutions that historically determined knowledge and research for generations. We need to create spaces in the academy where other ways of conducting research can be equally celebrated.

I started my doctoral studies in 2003 at the University of Auckland and was confirmed in May 2008. Although fairly new to academia, I have since worked in three universities including the University of Waikato (2007–2010), University of Canterbury (2011–2012) and now the University of Otago (2012 –present). People of influence who have significantly shaped my thinking and aspirations working in academia include Margie Hōhepa, Angus Macfarlane, Clive Aspin, Les Williams, Graham and Linda Smith, Clive Pope, Pip Ferguson, Alison Jones, Lucy Johnson, Mason Durie, Margaret Mutu and Selwyn Katene, all of whom work in mainstream universities and who remain good friends and colleagues to this day. Despite this support network, I would most certainly not be able to endure the challenges or highs and lows of working in academia without the love, patience and loyalty of my whānau. It is therefore no surprise that attempting to balance my career with the needs of whānau remains a key priority. Hard work, persistence and relationships are, I believe, the most important attributes to succeeding in academia. Indeed, it is not only gaining a PhD that qualifies one to work in academia, it is also about using the skills acquired to excel in academia – to publish, teach and to serve in the community.

Whānau perspectives of Māori academic leadership

From a whānau perspective, there are five concepts I wish to explore as being important to understanding how to lead, as distinct from notions of leadership. Manaia and Hona (2005) provide five themed concepts informed by the use of whakataukī.

1 Whakatutuki – acknowledging success

E kore te kūmara i whakapahu i tōna reka

The kūmara never tells how sweet it is

The proverb highlights the unassuming nature of Māori to be modest in the midst of achievement and that by nature Māori tend to acknowledge success as part of the wider collective of people, inclusive of iwi, hapū and whānau. From a personal perspective, it is expected that any success I derive from academia will also be of some benefit to my wider whānau and evidenced in their successes as much as my own.

2 Whakamana – earning respect

He tangata kī tahi

A person who speaks once

Traditionally, respect among Māori was derived from whakapapa, formalised by tikanga and defined by kawa (Manaia & Hona, 2005). The mana (status) of a people, however, was not so much derived from the deeds of an individual, but more so from the collective ability of the community to move together as one. Individually, to create offence is to create risk; to display arrogance invites retaliation; to demonstrate rudeness is to solicit insult; and to diminish others is to breed resentment. Such individual behaviours can be described as 'mana-mining' – acting for personal gain; 'mana-munching'– the act of ridiculing others; and 'mana-diminishing'– failing to be inclusive or reflective of the wider needs, sensitivities and aspirations of the tribe.

3 Te awe – influence

Ko te kai a te rangatira he kōrero

The food of chiefs is oratory

The past deeds of chiefs were often reflected in how effective they were at bringing people together to work. In an academic context, effective academic leaders have the ability to influence people to carry out tasks in ways that bring greater benefit to the collective group, whereby people are made to feel valued and appreciated. In my new role, a key goal is to capture the hearts and minds of people, to growing and developing the future of the Māori teacher education programme. Success breeds success, and in doing so, reveals the ability of a leader to enhance the capacity of people in close proximity to carry out tasks efficiently and successfully. The use of karakia, mōteatea, whakataukī, whakapapa and whakawhanaungatanga are all key elements of achieving ngā hononga or developing connectedness and synergies whenever people come together, and traditionally were highly valued in keeping a tribe connected.

4 Kaha me te kawe – power and responsibility

Mā te werawera o tōu mata e kai ai koe i te haunga ahi o te kai

By the perspiration on your face you will taste the piquant flavour of cooked food. Honest work brings its own reward.

Future Māori leaders must have an awareness and understanding of how power and responsibility operate within the world of Māori, and how to effectively manage each appropriately. Through demonstrating aroha, atawhai, whakaaetanga and whakapaitia, chiefs could navigate both as an expression of kotahitanga. Navigating the power relationships that exist in my new role requires that I share these values to offset personal egos that are likely to emerge as a result of competing values implicit within an institution's notions of individualism and accountability.

5 Mauri kaiārahi – Māori leadership values

Mā tini mā mano ka rapa te whai

By many, by thousands, the work (project) will be accomplished. Many hands make light work. Unity is strength.

Māori leadership is a difficult and challenging proposition to many who are often pitted against a range of institutional requirements. It is my intention in my new role to work hard and to always act with integrity, respect and kindness, but at the same time to be forthright in making decisions that will benefit the collective and enable Māori to foot it with their non-Māori counterparts. Moreover, accepting leadership roles in academia remains a challenging endeavour for many new and emerging Māori academic leaders, but is deeply necessary in helping to create and provide other spaces for Māori to fill over time. This also requires our current Māori leaders to promote a strong postgraduate culture as well as to develop other suitable career opportunities within academia.

Pursuit of balance in Māori academic leadership

In this final section I want to share four key attributes that I believe draw together many of the aforementioned ideas and that provide relevance to what we do as new and emerging Māori leaders. The following four attributes refer specifically to an inner ability to 'protect', 'problem solve', 'provide' and 'heal' in institutional spaces that are consistently changing, evolving and growing. The four attributes also complement our traditional intellectual wisdom that our connections to whānau, whakapapa and whenua sustain who we are and our place in the world. I also offer these attributes as a way of negotiating and navigating a 'common ground' between the values inherent in my identity and the values that underpin my new role as an Associate Professor in Māori teacher education. These four culturally connected attributes are inextricably linked to becoming an effective leader and can be applied in a number of different social-cultural contexts and at different times to achieve joy, harmony, peace and balance in our current roles in academia:

The ability to protect refers to ensuring we can 'maintain' who we are as Māori while remaining open to new knowledge, ways of thinking and doing.

The ability to problem solve refers to understanding how to make adjustments in times of adversity, challenge, hardship and struggle. A key aspect of being able to make the appropriate adjustments is our ability to be resilient, resistant, relevant and to draw strength from the collective (iwi, hapū and whānau).

The ability to provide refers to having access to a wide range of different resources, knowledge, networks and approaches that will help support not only our career aspirations, but equally our development as culturally connected human beings who care passionately about the impact our various roles will have on the lives of others and the communities we serve. This also requires creating the appropriate spaces, places and opportunities for Māori academics to work collaboratively and to share their work across different disciplines.

The ability to heal refers to Māori academic leaders having a level of autonomy and control, to be agents of change and to continue to learn and grow as cultural human beings.

A 'native' sense of knowing is also about enacting a culture of care based on the following cultural principles:

Manaakitanga: acknowledging the mana of others as having equal or greater importance than oneself by practising aroha (love of others), hospitality, generosity and mutual respect.

Rangatiratanga: weaving the people together with humility, generosity, diplomacy and knowledge that will benefit the people.

Whanaungatanga: engaging in the social organisation of whānau, hapū and iwi, including the rights and reciprocal obligations consistent with being part of a collective.

Kotahitanga: creating unity of purpose and direction.

Wairuatanga: generating the spiritual existence alongside the physical, expressed through the intimate connection of the people to their maunga, awa, moana and marae, and to tūpuna and atua.

Mana whenua: establishing tūrangawaewae and ūkaipō to enable people to belong, contribute and be valued.

Kaitiakitanga: being able to bring forth the spiritual and cultural guardianship of Te Ao Mārama (world of enlightenment) as part of our responsibility to care for others and the environment.

Mana Tupuna/Whakapapa: linking us to our ancestors and stories so that we can define our heritage and place in the world.

Te Reo Rangatira: readily using te reo Māori to explain the Māori world.

Pūkengatanga: becoming a repository of higher learning and scholarship.

Whirinakitanga: depending on and trusting one another.

Whakapono: demonstrating a belief in oneself.

Tūmanako: providing an ethos of hope.

Final thoughts

There is a real need to continue to find ways to foster and grow Māori academic leadership development across all universities in Aotearoa/New Zealand to ensure that our next group of Māori leaders in academia comes through. There can be no denying the fact that today's Māori academic leaders will need to have a doctorate, be active teachers and researchers and publish widely. At the same time, we also need a wider view of Māori leadership across all areas of society, including government, media, education, religion, business, research, science, local politics and, perhaps most importantly, the economy.

Perhaps a third of a leader's time should focus on learning the rules of how to become an effective leader in a mainstream tertiary institution; another third should be spent on actively engaging in what makes their research unique in the institution, school, college or faculty they choose to work in, so that their level of academic credibility is clearly visible; and finally, the remainder of their time should be spent on building the necessary networks, connections, interactions and sense of community to strengthen their role so that they can do their job even better.

Despite the various changes, challenges or issues we are likely to face in our various academic roles, my hope is that we do not lose sight of being leaders within our own whānau first. Moreover, being an effective leader is a lifelong commitment to people and those we are asked to serve. We also need to believe that despite the ongoing institutional pressures on existing Māori leaders, being able to stand as Māori first and foremost is a critical step in determining what type of leader we want to become. Suffice to say, leadership styles are just as diverse as the people who lead. On the other hand, not everyone is destined to lead and nor should we expect everyone to want to be involved in a leadership role. In many instances, leadership roles emerge because people actively and willingly accept this as part of their developing role.

At this time I am reminded of a recent movie my son Kainamu and I enjoyed watching called *Clash of the Titans* (2010), where Pegasus the mortal son (demi-god) of the god Zeus embarks on a perilous journey to stop Hades of the underworld and his minions from spreading their evil to Earth as well as the heavens. In Pegasus's eventual triumph over Hades in one of the many epic scenes (which by the way is so drowned in action and masculinity that it has something of a numbing effect), Pegasus turns to his remaining comrades saying, 'My father (mortal) was the only person I followed but due to what we have endured here today, I now follow you'. Of course if you have watched this movie to its conclusion you will know that Pegasus decides to stay on Earth and live out the rest of his life as a human being. A very noble decision, given that Pegasus could have easily chosen to live his life as a god alongside his father Zeus. Of course Zeus is equally happy about his son's decision and shows his acceptance of that decision by generously bringing back to life Pegasus's new love, who had died at the hands of Hades in one of the many epic struggles the movie portrays – a happy ending ultimately. The moral of the story is that good usually overcomes evil and if we remain resilient, courageous, and determined in times of hardship we can certainly overcome many of life's greatest challenges. Effective leaders in the modern era generally have the energy to keep focused on the vision and purpose of their calling, as well as to inspire others around them to take up the challenge, even the weary. Indeed, the movie teaches us to respect the higher order of life, and to listen carefully to our elders and their vision for us.

As academics, we may also need to consider, within our current role(s), how much are we prepared to give of ourselves for the 'greater good', including in relation to our innate responsibility to serve our iwi/hapū/whānau/marae? And indeed, working in academia, do we even know what the greater good we seek to serve is and how the time, effort and energy we give to an institution benefit our growth and development within a community setting? Subsequently, institutions expect academic staff, and especially senior academic staff, to teach, publish and serve on a number of committees and boards. Perhaps the greater good may well lie in what we do for each other, more so than what we think institutions expect of us in our current role(s). For many new and emerging Māori academics who like myself attended the Manu Ao leadership wānanga in 2010 and 2011, the jury is still out as to whether or not we consider ourselves as future Māori academic leaders; simply because, from a Māori world view perspective, the term 'leadership' tends to embrace a number of attributes that should be determined by the wider collective and not our own individual ambitions.

Finally, I want to leave you with the words of a (non-Māori) poet, Kelly D. Caron, who reflects on the importance of learning to trust yourself and to continue to aim high in everything you do:

Today's dreams are tomorrow's successes

Don't be afraid of high hopes
or plans that seem to be out of reach.
Life is meant to be experienced,
and every situation allows for
learning and growth.

Motivation is a positive starting point,
and action places you on a forward path.
A dream is a blueprint
of a goal not yet achieved;
the only difference between the two
is the effort involved in attaining
what you hope to accomplish.

Let your mind and heart urge you on;
allow the power of your will
to lead you to your destination.

Don't count the steps ahead;
just add up the total
of steps already covered,
and multiply it by
faith, confidence, and endurance.

Always remember that
for those who persist,
today's dreams are transformed
into tomorrow's successes. (Caron, n.d.)

Kia kaha, kia māia, kia manawanui – mauri ora rangatira mā!

REFERENCES

Cammock, P. (2001). *The Dance of Leadership: The call for soul in 21st century leadership.* Auckland, New Zealand: Pearson Education.

Caron, K.D. (n.d.). 'Today's dreams are tomorrow's successes.' Retrieved 3 September 2012 from: http://www.cybernation.com/victory/youcandoit/poems.php#poem14

Graen, G.B. & Hui, C. (1999). 'Transcultural global leadership in the twenty-first century: Challenges and implications for development.' In W.H. Mobley (ed.), *Advances in Global Leadership* (pp. 9–26). Stamford, CT: JAI Press.

Katene, S. (2010). 'Modelling Māori leadership: What makes for good leadership?' *MAI Review, 2.* Retrieved 3 September 2012 from: http://www.review.mai.ac.nz/index.php/MR/article/view/334

Jahnke, H.T. (2008, 9 November). 'The task of an educator is supporting "communities of learners" as transformative praxis.' Keynote presentation at the Association of Tertiary Learning Advisors of Aotearoa New Zealand (ATLAANZ) Conference, Whitireia Community Polytechnic, Porirua, New Zealand.

Manaia, W. & Hona, D. (2005). 'The changing face of Māori development: Mauri Kaiārahi – Māori leadership values'. Presented at the First Foundation Young Māori Leaders' Conference. Retrieved 3 September 2012 from: http://www.firstfound.org/manaia%20and%20hona.htm

Mead, H.M. (1997). *Ngā Toi Māori: Māori art on the world scene.* Wellington, New Zealand: Ahua Design and Illustration/Matau Associates.

Mead, H., Stevens, S., Third, J., Jackson, B. & Pfeifer, D. (2005). 'Hui Taumata Leadership in Governance Scoping Paper: Māori leadership in governance.' Victoria University of Wellington, Wellington, New Zealand. Retrieved 3 September 2012 from: http://www.huitaumata.Māori.nz/pdf/leadershipingovernance.pdf.

Parry, K.W. (1996). *Transformational Leadership: Developing an enterprising management culture.* Melbourne: Pitman Publishing.

CHAPTER **8**

Mahitahi: Interconnectedness and leading together

Phillipa Pehi and Reremoana Theodore

Introduction

Our vision for the future of Māori academic leadership is based on the idea of interconnectedness and values associated with working together (mahitahi). The idea that we are all connected is linked to the principles of collective leadership. This chapter is based on our beliefs and perspectives as emerging Māori academics, and in particular our own experiences within academia. We focus particularly on the sharing of, collective participation in, and contribution to, the processes and acts of leadership. These processes are examined in the light of some challenges facing emerging Māori academic leadership, including power and privilege, dealing with conflict, having courage and being true to oneself. We also discuss the role of soul, heart and spirit in relation to leadership. Finally, we reflect on our future as Māori academics in relation to dealing with fear, and cultivating hope, faith and love.

Interconnectedness

Interconnectedness – that all things in creation are connected to one another – is a basic tenet of many Indigenous cultures (Marsden, 1975; Kawagley, 1995; Andrade, 2008). What one does in the web of life naturally and unavoidably radiates out to the rest of creation (Knudtson & Suzuki, 1992). Following this train of thought, the actions that one individual takes will impact on other people (and non-humans), and vice versa. This is a sobering thought when we consider how our behaviours, thoughts and beliefs affect the world around us, including its other inhabitants, for example, the extinction of species and the destruction of forests (Shiva, 1998). In contrast, our modern-day society has been described as operating from a different world view. People are seen as individuals who operate autonomously and with minimal regard to how others may be affected by their actions (Marsden, 1975; Jensen & Draffan, 2003).

These two differing approaches to life may also affect how leadership is viewed and enacted. In the past, much has been written about leadership both nationally and internationally, and there are multiple theories and definitions of leadership (Avolio, Walumbwa & Weber, 2009). Books and articles have been written about past and present Māori leaders, and more recently Māori academic leadership (Katene, 2010; Matthews, 2011). From many Indigenous perspectives, leadership studies would involve an in-depth evaluation of how people are involved in the process of leadership through a series of choices and actions; and how others are affected by those people (and the environments) around them (Benham & Murakami-Ramalho, 2010; White, 2010). Therefore the process of relating and having relationships (whakawhanaungatanga) (Fitzgerald, 2003) is understood as being important, with leadership practices being embedded in a system of interdependencies (Fletcher & Käufer, 2003).

From this point of view, the notion of one single leader seems at odds with the idea of interconnectedness, because very rarely does leadership involve the actions of one single person. However, modern views of leadership often focus on the achievements or characteristics of a single person (or a small group of people), with other people viewed as followers (Crevani, Lindgren & Packendorff, 2007). This perspective is one where those other than the leader are seen to be acted upon. As we will discuss in later sections, this more individualistic approach has markedly different outcomes for leaders and followers, usually resulting in greater positive outcomes for those at the top and progressively fewer benefits for those further down the hierarchy (Hollander, 1992).

Difficulties in dealing with different leadership principles and approaches may be seen to arise from dual expectations stemming from these different world views. These difficulties can be particularly apparent for Māori and Indigenous academics, undertaking research and work at the interface between different knowledge systems, for example, science and mātauranga Māori (Durie, 2004; Hikuroa, Slade & Gravley, 2011), where they are expected to successfully navigate and integrate these different ways of being and doing, for example, community vs university practices. These problems may be compounded if one world view is privileged over another (Jensen & Draffan, 2003). From our perspective, highlighting and promoting the benefits from collective leadership approaches may help us navigate a way forward. As we discuss in further detail, this type of leadership may also help us as academics to better address issues such as working to improve the health and well-being of our environment and people.

Leading together

There has been much written about individual leaders and their lives. Many of our personal heroes include such international leaders as Nelson Mandela, Gandhi and Mother Teresa. Past Māori leaders have also been recognised and acknowledged for their role in changing and improving the lives of others, including visionaries like Dame Whina Cooper and Erihapeti Rehu-Murchie. A number of present-day, individually recognised academic Māori leaders, for example, Sir Mason Durie and Professor Linda Tuhiwai Smith, have also worked to create better lives for Māori and their whānau. These leaders have assumed the mantle of public leadership and provide us with examples of effective Māori leadership.

These Māori leaders would likely be the first to acknowledge, however, that their success rests with the endeavours of many, and not only themselves. When we focus too much on individual leaders, we can lessen the importance of the group, which may result in a number of issues for us as a collective. Firstly, it makes it easier to blame a leader or small leadership team when things fail (Yuki, 1999). This process allows a certain level of abdication of personal responsibility by each individual for their role in the project or situation. Alternatively, this approach to leadership also means that only individuals are acknowledged when projects succeed. Another issue is related to organisational structures, which in the last hundred years have resulted in hierarchies of management and more distinct divisions of labour (Seers, Keller & Wilkerson, 2003). Management hierarchies exist within New Zealand universities, with leadership roles generally being assigned (and accepted as belonging) to those individuals at higher levels of the hierarchy, that is, Professor, or Dean of School. The expertise and wisdom of those within leadership positions is important to acknowledge. If these roles are too strictly adhered to, however, they may affect the group and its work in a negative way, for example, stifling innovation among junior members. In comparison, the ideals of collective leadership and endeavour require that leadership be acknowledged in each and every person.

A more collective response to leadership may not only help within an academic environment but it could also help to address larger societal issues through the recognition that leadership is a universal process affecting all areas of our public and personal lives (Cammock, 2003). Moreover, Lambert (2002) describes the importance of 'acts of leadership' and recognises that everyone has the ability, right and responsibility to be a leader. Recognising the nature of interconnectedness through collective approaches could help to place academia and leadership back within communities and the rest of the world (DePaola, 1999). Collective approaches by their very nature necessitate the recognition that we are all in this world together and that divisions are merely the constructs we choose to put upon ourselves and the world around us.

Our ideas about collective leadership are not only about leadership specifically, but also the values related to working and living together, for example, manaakitanga and kotahitanga. The ideal of a collective way of being honours interconnectedness, for example, by supporting the less fortunate by sharing the benefits of collective work in order to strengthen the whole (Tuara, 1992; Te Rito, 2006). In the world at large (and for Māori specifically), the social, political, environmental and health issues, for example, poverty, chronic disease and climate change, that we collectively face can at times seem overwhelming (Durie, 2011). These issues have resulted in part through historical injustices, for example land confiscation, and are often due to influences outside of our individual control, such as legislation (Bishop, 2003; Robson & Harris, 2007). These issues are too unwieldy and complex to rest on the shoulders of a few. To address these concerns adequately requires the recognition and contribution of many people's different skill sets, strengths, knowledge and abilities (Nairn, Pehi, Black & Waitoki, 2012).

A more collective approach to leadership may help to uncover new solutions and also improve the lives of all those actively involved. For contribution to encourage and foster well-being, we believe that people need to feel that what they bring to the table is worthwhile, and that their contribution is valued and respected. This acknowledgement by others may help people to feel needed, included, and as if they have a place to belong (Pehi, 2005; Garner, 2009).

This type of leadership is described in the work undertaken by the whānau at Te Kōpae Piripono, a Māori immersion early childhood education centre in Taranaki (Te Kōpae Piripono, 2008). They view leadership (which they define as 'Mana Tangata') in relation to four pledges, 'Ngā Takohanga e Whā'. These pledges are having responsibility, taking responsibility, sharing responsibility and being responsible. In their research on whānau development, they found that Ngā Takohanga e Whā, empathy, support and persistence were important for encouraging and supporting whānau participation, development and learning in education.

Power and privilege

A change in perspective may be required from those who already have power (i.e. money, resources, knowledge), influence and privilege in order for collective or shared leadership approaches to exist within modern institutional structures such as universities. In his book on meeting the ethical challenges of leadership, Johnson (2012) argues that leaders almost always enjoy greater privileges than followers, which may lead to the abuse of power. Furthermore, despite many people being uncomfortable with the fact that modern-day leadership does not exist without power, we should recognise the corrosive impact that power can have on the people who possess it (Needham, 2008). Ignoring or demonising the topic of power may also be problematic, especially when power can be used to help others, for example, enlisting the support of local groups to raise funds, or helping communities to petition politicians and policy makers (Johnson, 2012).

Creating leadership that allows for the contribution of all people involved may be difficult within a society where decision-making abilities increase the higher an individual's position or status. Couple this leadership style with systems that are time and resource poor (and are therefore seeking to cut corners where possible), enabling contribution may be either passively or actively avoided, such as in the case of consultation with stakeholders within resource management (Mutu, 2002).

Within our society, academics hold positions of power and privilege and our views and opinions are often validated through our qualifications and our knowledge in certain areas. Academics can play an important role within society through teaching, research and community service. However, the negative impact that academia and research have had on community and Indigenous peoples has been documented by a number of authors (Smith, 1999; Cochran et al., 2008). Historically in New Zealand, conventional Western scientific and ethical frameworks have tended to position Māori as passive subjects of research who are 'researched upon' (Kennedy & Cram, 2010). As a result, many have worked to validate Māori knowledge and world views within academia and have highlighted the importance of Māori leading and having meaningful participation in research (Pohatu, 2003; Hudson & Russell, 2009).

As Māori, we are not immune to the human negative aspects and behaviours, for example, bullying, that either wanting or holding power and privilege can lead to within these institutions. This situation is particularly poignant because of our collective history of the denigration and destruction of Māori autonomy or self-governance (Walker, 1990). In our careers as emerging academics, we have seen the negative impact that workplace bullying has on individuals and teams. Workplace bullying has been described as 'something that someone repeatedly does or says to gain power or dominance over another, including any action or implied action, such as threats, intended to cause fear and distress' (Evans v Gen-i Limited, 2005). One key aspect of workplace bullying occurs when those in power act in a way that blocks the sharing of leadership roles and responsibilities (and the privileges and opportunities), or fails to acknowledge the other members of a team or their contributions (Needham, 2008).

To deal with the negative aspects of power and privilege requires collective leadership behaviours and mechanisms to be put in place. Four strategies that we believe are effective are: viewing leadership as service; humility; showing appreciation; and surrounding yourself with people who help you to 'keep it real'. Firstly, sharing leadership is related to the idea of leadership as service to others (Russell, 2001). When we see leadership roles as ones in which we serve and help others, then we are less likely to be caught up in trying to have or maintain power over others. Secondly, humility is an important trait to cultivate in relation to leadership and has been described as being made up of three components that help leaders to build relationships and foster collaboration and trust: self-awareness; openness; and transcendence (acknowledging a power greater than the self) (Johnson, 2012). Thirdly, showing appreciation is an important aspect of leadership and is derived from the Latin meaning to 'place a value on' (Cammock, 2003). Very little time is required to show one's appreciation and yet it can have a positive effect not just on the individuals who are singled out but on overall group harmony as well, as group members want to contribute more to the group in terms of their time and effort. Importantly, being appreciated may give members within a group a sense of belonging and value, and increase their sense of connection to the project, place, group or situation (Pehi, 2005). Finally, whānau, supervisors, mentors, students and friends all help us as academics to be leaders, commonly through the advice, solace, help and encouragement often given in private. Having friends who provide honest feedback (both good and bad) is crucial in our opinion. Children also play an important role in leadership. In our own lives, children have helped us to 'keep it real'; as there is often not too much glory (although sometimes pride) in successfully changing a nappy, settling an argument between siblings, dealing with tantrums and doing basic housework. Children are also a constant reminder of what is important and why many of us academics do the mahi (work) that we do. As the Ngāi Tahu whakataukī says: 'Mō tātou, ā, mō kā uri ā muri ake nei' – 'For us and our children after us' (Te Rūnanga o Ngāi Tahu, 2009).

Conflict and courage

As Māori, we often have differences of opinion or have different ways of doing things. These differences reflect the great diversity within Māori. Far from being a homogenous group, Māori pre-colonisation were made up of diverse, self-identified whānau and hapū with different ways of being (Walker, 1990). Indeed the term Māori was not used by Māori to refer to themselves prior to colonisation, and was simply a term used to denote things as 'normal' (Ihimaera, 1998). In modern times, our different points of focus, skill sets and upbringings (e.g. rural vs urban) further increase the variety between us as a people.

Understanding and respecting another person's contribution may help us to deal with differences and disagreements when they arise. In our academic careers, we have both felt pain and sadness when disagreements have created unresolved conflict, group disharmony and a feeling of not belonging to the group. When we reflect on our experiences, we have found that recognising another person's abilities and mahi and not blocking the contribution they make (despite personal resentments or hurt), has helped us to heal personally, and has also worked to the benefit of the collective. In accepting their contribution, we accept their human-ness (i.e. the 'good' along with the 'bad') and also their ability to change. This in turn makes it easier to forgive ourselves when we make mistakes and are 'human' too. From this perspective, while disagreements and even conflict can be regarded as perhaps an unavoidable consequence of diverse people working together, the end result need not be negative (Tau, 2012).

Allowing contribution does not mean that we do not speak up or take action when we disagree with what another person (or group) is saying or doing. Taking action requires courage, a key leadership quality that has been described as the ability to overcome fear in order to do the right thing (Johnson, 2012). Leaving a group may be difficult, in part because of the powerful human need to belong. Positive group membership and belonging can provide us with meaning and purpose. Belonging to a group, and the identity that comes with that group membership, can give us a sense of strength from which to contribute (Pehi, 2005). However, sometimes the sacrifice of attaining or maintaining group membership may be harmful to our own development or inhibit our potential to become more fully ourselves (Palmer, 2000).

Importantly, being true to oneself can also be an act of courage. In his book *The Element*, Ken Robinson (2009) eloquently captures this idea:

> One of the strongest signs of being in the zone is a sense of freedom and of authenticity. When we are doing something that we love and are naturally good at, we are much more likely to feel centered in our true sense of self – to be who we feel we truly are. When we are in our Element, we feel we are doing what we are meant to be doing and being who we're meant to be. (p. 90)

Robinson describes 'the Element' as being the place where the things that we love to do and the things that we are good at come together. As we learn to be true to ourselves, we feel more at peace and we may also be able to allow others to be themselves without judging their motives or choices (Palmer, 2000).

Soul, heart and spirit

In *The Dance of Leadership*, Peter Cammock (2003) calls for soul in twenty-first century leadership. He argues that leadership requires more than skill: it also requires emotion, identity and character, which are traditionally associated with the soul (moral, spiritual and emotional forces). Recently, academia has been criticised for negatively influencing education as a whole, because it has tended to push aside any activity that involves heart, emotions, the body or our senses (Robinson, 2009). This causes problems, particularly as wherever there are humans, you will find emotion also. In the current climate within academia that requires collective endeavour (e.g. multidisciplinary and transdisciplinary collaboration), quality relationships between people may be essential in whether efforts are successful or not. We believe that successful academic leadership requires high emotional intelligence (Salovey & Mayer, 1990) as well as intellect – in other words, people who are able to use their feelings (i.e. empathy) as well as their thoughts to connect with others. Furthermore, leadership to create positive change requires heart. It requires aroha (Te Momo, 2011).

At present, the leaders of our country are focused heavily on economic growth, in part due to the recent global financial crisis (New Zealand Treasury, 2012). As academics, this affects us because we are reliant on governmental funding to undertake our mahi. Moreover, funding within educational institutions is associated with governmental priorities. In the Ministry of Education's Statement of Intent 2012–2017 (2012), two priorities were identified: improving educational outcomes for Māori learners, Pasifika learners, learners with special education needs and learners from low socio-economic backgrounds; and maximising the contribution of education to the New Zealand economy. For Māori, the first priority is extremely important. The second priority is also important, as improving the nation's economy will be related to employment opportunities, technological advancements, commercial innovation and wealth creation. However, as we look forward another hundred years we are aware that past economic gains have not been distributed equally within our society, and some of these gains have been made at the expense of vital aspects of Māori culture such as the environment, for example, widespread degradation of waterways (PCE, 1998). At present, worldwide occupation and environmental protests (Hardt & Negri, 2011) recognise these disparities in relation to the distribution of wealth and resources, and have focused on social, environmental and economic inequalities, greed, corruption and the pervasive influence of corporations on government.

We would argue that concerns regarding short-term budgets and bottom-line economics must also be coupled with our deeper set of values, ethics and morals and the spirit in which we are trying to reduce social disparities and ethnic inequalities to create positive change and outcomes. As described by Dame Anne Salmond in the *New Zealand Herald* (Salmond, 2011), there is more to securing our future than just technological and commercial innovation, but at the very least our land, sea and young people must be cared for. However economic 'development' remains at the forefront of most government agendas globally, including that of New Zealand (Jensen & Draffan, 2003). This almost exclusive focus often denies the reality of the human and non-human casualties left in the wake of such economic exploitation (Shiva, 1998).

In addition to the values of having soul and heart in leadership, we believe that it is important to acknowledge the role that spirituality can play. Spirituality is often thought to be at odds with academic practice, particularly with scientific study. However, there is now considerable research interest in this area and the number of academic articles on spirituality in the workplace has increased dramatically over the last two decades (Johnson, 2012). Within our own lives, spirituality has played an important role both inside and outside of academia. Spiritual practice such as prayer, yoga and meditation has helped us to make meaning of our lives and experiences; deal with problems and adversity; and maintain a level of balance, thereby improving our health and well-being. Moreover, our spirituality is strongly informed by our beliefs and practices as Māori, for example, karakia, tohu, matakite.

Visioning the future: hope, faith and love

We believe that Māori academic leadership (or any leadership for that matter), whether it is acknowledged or not, is a collective endeavour. This understanding stems from the belief that all things in life are interconnected. Therefore our work and achievements are a culmination of choices and actions made by ourselves and many other people. Whether we live in harmony with this one idea (or not) could determine how well we live, work and lead together. The ideas of interconnectedness and leading together mean that we can all be viewed as leaders. The problem for the future, however, may reside in our reluctance to accept that leadership requires something of us in return. This is the subject of this final section.

Leadership often requires us to face a number of our fears. In this chapter we have already written about fear in relation to having courage. Facing fears can be a part of our professional and personal lives (Jeffers, 1987). We face the fear of criticism, failure, success, not fitting in and/or being found wanting. One way we suggest collective leadership can help us deal with these fears is to accept that as part of a group of academic leaders, we can share among ourselves the responsibility of leadership. No longer do we have to be the leader, or the expert. We can give ourselves permission to learn and make mistakes, to grow and develop alongside our colleagues.

Another fear can arise when we become aware that the way we humans are living today will negatively impact on our futures, for example, environmental issues (Jensen & Draffan, 2003; Shiva, 1998), and we cannot envision another way to be in the world. Along with having the courage to open our eyes and to make desired changes in our own lives, we need to have and demonstrate hope, faith, and love that we can (through our individual and collective actions) make this world a better place. Working collectively requires a large degree of both tolerance and respect for others and their different ways of being in the world. Love for others, as well as showing faith and hope in them and their abilities, can help, though anyone who has attempted collective endeavours knows this is not always an easy task to achieve.

Hope has been defined as allowing for (and preferring) the possibility for things to change or become better. Faith on the other hand is the knowledge that things will change for the better (Moore, 1992). Faith and hope can help us to face the future with positivity and optimism despite present levels of adversity, crises and disparities. To have faith and hope enables us to deal with challenges such as cynicism, criticism and self-doubt. These qualities also enable future visioning, which requires the ability to look beyond current realities and feelings of powerlessness to engage in vigorous future imagining (Durie, 2011). As stated earlier, a Māori world view emphasises the need to focus on living in the world in a manner that ensures a healthy future for our mokopuna and those generations that follow (Kennedy & Jefferies, 2009). Other Indigenous peoples also talk of the future as one in which 'we borrow the earth from our children', and the importance of plans for the future visioning at least 'seven generations' into the future (The Harvard Project on American Indian Economic Development, 2008).

Earlier in the chapter we discussed the importance of having heart in relation to leadership. Aroha is described by Rev. Māori Marsden as the essence from which all creation stems and as the most important mana in the world (Royal, 2003). Aroha is wholeness (Royal, 2006). Love is a universal theme and is referenced throughout recorded human history through all religions, cultures and societies. In remembering our shared humanity (with all our strengths and weaknesses), we have discovered that aroha (for both ourselves and others), is a key ingredient from which flows (among many things) humility, appreciation, being of service, having courage, facing fears and working together.

Through our experience as emerging Māori academics, we have identified for ourselves ways of being that enable us to work, live and lead more collectively, and have shared them in this chapter. We believe that all these factors contribute to enduring relationships that form the foundations for lifelong (sometimes generations-long) collective endeavours. We acknowledge this is a lofty ideal, but one which we can vision and continue to work towards as a pathway for a better life for ourselves and for those still to come.

REFERENCES

Andrade, C. (2008). *Hā'ena: Through the eyes of the ancestors.* Honolulu: University of Hawai'i Press.

Avolio, B.J., Walumbwa, F.O. & Weber, T.J. (2009). 'Leadership: current theories, research and future directions.' *Annual Review of Psychology, 60*, 421–49.

Benham, M. & Murakami-Ramalho, E. (2010). 'Engaging in educational leadership: the generosity of spirit.' *International Journal of Leadership in Education: Theory and Practice, 13*(1), 77–91.

Bess, J.L. & Goldman, P. (2001). 'Leadership ambiguity in universities and K-12 schools and the limits of contemporary leadership theory.' *The Leadership Quarterly, 12*(4), 419–50.

Bishop, R. (2003). 'Changing power relations in education: kaupapa Māori messages for "mainstream" education in Aotearoa/New Zealand.' *Comparative Education, 39*(2), 221–38.

Cammock, P. (2003). *The Dance of Leadership: The call for soul in 21st century leadership* (2nd edn). Auckland, New Zealand: Prentice Hall.

Cochran, P.A.L., Marshall, C.A., Garcia-Downing, C., Kendall, E., Cook, D., McCubbin, L. & Gover, R.M.S. (2008). 'Indigenous ways of knowing: implications for participatory research and community.' *American Journal of Public Health, 98*(1), 22–27. doi: 10.2105/ AJPH.2006.093641

Crevani, L., Lindgren, M. & Packendorff, J. (2007). 'Shared leadership: a postheroic perspective on leadership as a collective construction.' *International Journal of Leadership Studies, 3*(1), 40–67.

DePaola, D.P. (1999). 'Beyond the university: leadership for the common good.' In *Leadership for the Future: The dental school in the university.* Washington, DC: American Association of Dental Schools.

Durie, M. (2004). 'Understanding health and illness: research at the interface between science and indigenous knowledge.' *International Journal of Epidemiology, 33*, 1138–43.

Durie, M. (2011). *Ngā Tini Whetū: Navigating Māori futures.* Wellington, New Zealand: Huia Publishers.

Evans v Gen-i Limited unreported, D. King, 29 August 2005, AA 333/05.

Fitzgerald, T. (2003). 'Interrogating orthodox voices: gender, ethnicity and educational leadership.' *School Leadership & Management* (formerly *School Organisation*), *23*(4), 431–44.

Fletcher, J.K. & Käufer, K. (2003). 'Shared leadership: paradox and possibility.' In C.L. Pearce & J.A. Conger (eds), *Shared Leadership: Reframing the hows and whys of leadership* (pp. 21–47). Thousand Oaks, CA: Sage Publications.

Garner, G. (2009). 'Belonging and acknowledgement: discussing community-based arts projects with Shahin Shafaei.' *Migration Action, 1*, 30–31.

Hardt, M. & Negri, A. (2011). 'The fight for "real democracy" at the heart of Occupy Wall Street.' *Foreign Affairs*. Retrieved from: www.foreignaffairs.com/articles/136399/michael-hardt-and-antonionegri/the-fight-for-real-democracy-at-the-heart-of-occupy-wall-street

Hikuroa, D., Slade, A. & Gravley, D. (2011). 'Implementing Māori indigenous knowledge (Mātauranga) in a scientific paradigm: restoring the mauri to Te Kete Poutama.' *MAI Review, 3*. Retrieved from: http://www.review.mai.ac.nz/index.php/MR/article/view/433

Hollander, E.P. (1992). 'Ethical challenges in the leader-follower relationship.' *Business Ethics Quarterly, 5*(1), 55–65.

Hudson, M.L. & Russell, K. (2009). 'The Treaty of Waitangi and research ethics in Aotearoa.' *Journal of Bioethical Inquiry, 6*(1), 61–68. doi: 10.1007/s11673-008-9127-0.

Ihimaera, W. (ed.) (1998). *Growing up Māori*. Auckland, New Zealand: Tandem Press.

Jeffers, S. (1987). *Feel the Fear and Do It Anyway*. New York, NY: Fawcett Columbine.

Jensen, D. & Draffan, G. (2003). *Strangely Like War: The global assault on forests*. Devon, UK: Green Books.

Johnson, C.E. (2001). *Meeting the Ethical Challenges of Leadership: Casting light or shadow* (4th edn). Los Angeles, CA: Sage Publications.

Katene, S. (2010). 'Modelling Māori leadership: what makes for good leadership.' *MAI Review, 2*. Retrieved from: http://www.review.mai.ac.nz/index.php/MR/article/view/334

Kawagley, A.O. (1995). *A Yupiaq Worldview: A pathway to ecology and spirit*. Illinois: Waveland Press.

Kennedy, N. & Jefferies, R. (2009). 'Māori outcome evaluation (MOE): a kaupapa Māori environmental outcomes and indicators framework and methodology.' Planning Under Co-operative Mandates (PUCM) Māori Report 1, The International Global Change Institute (IGCI), Hamilton.

Kennedy, V. & Cram, F. (2010). 'Ethics of researching with whānau collectives.' *MAI Review, 3*. Retrieved from: www.review.mai.ac.nz/index.php/MR/article/viewFile/381/560

Knudtson, P. & Suzuki, D. (1992). *Wisdom of the Elders: Sacred native stories of nature*. New York, NY: Stoddart.

Marsden, M. (1975). 'God, man and universe: a Māori view.' In M. King (ed.), *Te Ao Hurihuri: The world moves on* (pp. 191–219). Wellington, New Zealand: Hicks, Smith & Sons.

Matthews, N. (2011). 'Reflecting on Māori academic leadership.' *MAI Review, 3*, Leadership Reflections. Retrieved from: http://www.review.mai.ac.nz/index.php/MR/article/view/457

Ministry of Education (2012). *Statement of Intent 2012–2017*. Wellington, New Zealand: New Zealand Government. Retrieved from: http://www.minedu.govt.nz/~/media/MinEdu/Files/TheMinistry/2012SOI/2012StatementOfIntent.pdf

Moore, T. (1992). *Care of the Soul: A guide for cultivating depth and sacredness in everyday life*. New York, NY: HarperCollins.

Mutu, M. (2002). 'Barriers to Tangata Whenua participation in resource management.' In M. Kawharu (ed.), *Whenua: Managing our resources* (pp. 75–95). Auckland, New Zealand: Reed.

Nairn, R., Pehi, P., Black, R. & Waitoki, W. (eds) (2012). *Ka Tū, Ka Oho: Visions of a bicultural partnership in Psychology (Invited keynotes: revisiting the past to reset the future)* (pp. 13–26). Wellington, New Zealand: New Zealand Psychological Society.

Needham, A.W. (2008). *Courage at the Top: Igniting the leadership fire.* Auckland, New Zealand: Penguin Books.

New Zealand Treasury (2012). *New Zealand: Economic and financial overview 2012.* Wellington, New Zealand: New Zealand Government. Retrieved from: http://www. treasury.govt.nz/economy/overview/2012/nzefo-12.pdf.

Palmer, P.J. (2000). *Let Your Life Speak: Listening for the voice of vocation.* San Francisco, CA: John Wiley & Sons.

Parliamentary Commissioner for the Environment (PCE) (1998). *Kaitiakitanga and Local Government: Tangata whenua participation in environmental management.* Wellington, New Zealand: Parliamentary Commissioner for the Environment.

Pehi, P. (2005). 'Intergroup discrimination and the need to belong.' Doctoral thesis, University of Otago, Dunedin, New Zealand.

Pohatu, T.W. (2003). 'Ata: growing respectful relationships.' Retrieved from: http://www. kaupapamāori.com/assets/ata.pdf

Robinson, K. (2009*). The Element: How finding your passion changes everything.* London, UK: Penguin Books.

Robson, B. & Harris, R. (eds) (2007). *Hauora: Māori Standards of Health IV. A study of the Years 2000–2005.* Wellington, New Zealand: Te Rōpū Rangahau Hauora a Eru Pōmare.

Royal, Te A.C. (ed.) (2003). *The Woven Universe: Selected writings of the Reverend Māori Marsden.* Kaitaia, New Zealand: Estate of the Reverend Māori Marsden.

Royal, Te A.C. (2006). *Te Ngākau.* Wellington, New Zealand: Mauriora Ki Te Ao.

Russell, R.F. (2001). 'The role of values in servant leadership.' *Leadership & Organization Development Journal, 22*(2), 76–84.

Salmond, A. (2011, October 18). 'Dame Anne Salmond: we could do with a change of heart.' *New Zealand Herald.* Retrieved from: http://www.nzherald.co.nz/nz/news/article. cfm?c_id=1&objectid=10759752

Salovey, P. & Mayer, J.D. (1990). 'Emotional intelligence.' *Imagination, Cognition and Personality, 9,* 185–211.

Seers, A., Keller, T. & Wilkerson, J.M. (2003). 'Can team members share leadership: foundations in research and teaching.' In *Shared Leadership: Reframing the hows and whys of leadership.* California: Sage Publications.

Shiva, V. (1998). *The Plunder of Nature and Knowledge.* Cambridge: South End Press.

Smith, L.T. (2012). *Decolonizing Methodologies: Research and indigenous peoples.* Dunedin, New Zealand: University of Otago Press/Zed Books.

Tau, Te M. (2012). 'Culture – thinking, doing and meaning.' In Nairn, R., Pehi, P., Black, R. & Waitoki, W. (eds), *Ka Tū, Ka Oho: Visions of a bicultural partnership in Psychology (Invited keynotes: revisiting the past to reset the future)* (pp. 171–93). Wellington, New Zealand: New Zealand Psychological Society.

Te Kōpae Piripono (2008). 'Ko koe kei tēnā kīwai, ko au kei tēnei kīwai o te kete (You carry your handle and I'll carry my handle, of our kete).' *Education Counts.* Wellington, New Zealand: New Zealand Government. Retrieved from: http://www.educationcounts.govt. nz/publications/ece/22551/34825/34830

Te Momo, O.F. (2011). 'Whakanekeneke rangatira: evolving leadership.' *MAI Review, 2*. Retrieved from: http://www.review.mai.ac.nz/index.php/MR/article/view/437

Te Rito, P. (2006). 'Leadership in Māori, European cultures and in the world of sport.' Intern Research Report 8. *MAI Review, 1*. Retrieved from: http://ojs.review.mai.ac.nz/index. php/MR/article/view/79

Te Rūnanga o Ngāi Tahu (2009). *Annual Report*. Retrieved from: http://www.Ngāitahu.iwi. nz/Publications/AnnualReports/2009/TinoRangatiratanga.php

The Harvard Project on American Indian Economic Development (2008). *The State of the Native Nations: Conditions under U.S. policies of self-determination*. New York: Oxford University Press.

Tuara, N. (1992). *Ngā Toka Tū Moana: Māori leadership and decision making*. Wellington, New Zealand: Te Puni Kōkiri.

Walker, R.J. (1990). *Ka Whawhai Tonu Mātou: Struggle without end*. Auckland, New Zealand: Penguin.

White, N. (2010), 'Indigenous Australian women's leadership: stayin' strong against the post-colonial tide.' *International Journal of Leadership in Education: Theory and Practice, 13*(1), 7–25.

Yuki, G. (1999). 'An evaluation of conceptual weaknesses in transformational and charismatic leadership theories.' *The Leadership Quarterly, 10*(2), 285–305.

CHAPTER **9**

Kaitiakitanga as Environmental Leadership

Margaret Forster

Introduction

In writing this letter it is intended to illustrate the significant cultural values that the tangata whenua have for the Whakakī Lagoon ... In the days of our forefathers and to the present day, the great lake has been a major source of food. There were eels in great numbers which were caught from February to May, processed and preserved for the leaner months of winter ... [at] the Pātangata end of the lake, there were flounders, herrings, mullet, whitebait, pipi, and ngūpara ... There were also the pārera, wana, pūkeko, matuku and other birds ...

This has now changed drastically due to the ecosystem being muddled with by engineers who could not, by any stretch of the imagination, envisage the result ... The food source which the people of Whakakī relied on for many generations has now almost disappeared, perhaps we should be thankful for the meagre catches of eels we get. No longer can we go to Paka or Pātangata to set out eel pā's [weirs] or go around the sandy stretches to spear flounder, or set a net to catch herrings.

The river, where we once swam as children, has now silted up. We could row from Pātangata to the lake and up to Te Ewe to the marae in canoes, a feat which is now impossible. Our mothers and grandmothers used to spend their days sitting in these canoes netting whitebait in season or at night bobbing for eels.

The tangata whenua of Whakakī desired a total way of life from this lagoon and its tributaries. Their ancestors are buried in several urupā around the perimeters of the lagoons. The spiritual connections are strongly bonded between the land, lagoons and people. The heritage bonds give the tangata whenua their pride, their mana and their spiritual culture.

The cultural aspects that stemmed from living around the lagoons was a way of life and the handing down of traditions from the older generations. The gathering, processing and storage of food was of a total involvement and shared responsibility. This brought about a pride in a heritage that was unique to the people of the area. The shared responsibility gave opportunity for the elders to relate traditions as well as sharing their expertise and knowledge. This continues to happen to this day, with adaptations to suit modern storage equipment.

In these changing times where a natural order of nature is fast disappearing, we as kai tiaki (Trustees) of the environment should endeavour to maintain all natural resources. This is to ensure that future generations can grow up with a heritage that is a vital part of being Māori.

(Letter written 25 May 1992 from kaumatua Huki Solomon to the Parliamentary Commissioner Helen Hughes)

In exploring the question of what is Māori leadership I could have begun with a series of definitions. Alternatively, I could have identified prominent Māori leaders such as Te Puea Herangi and described those traits of leadership valued by Māori society. I choose not to take this approach. Rather, this exploration of leadership begins with a letter, a simple narrative that, in my opinion, captures the essence of environmental leadership.

The letter that opened this chapter was written by kaumatua Huki Solomon, a prominent leader of the Māori community at Whakakī, to the Parliamentary Commissioner for the Environment (PCE) Helen Hughes. The local hapū Ngāti Hine, Ngāti Hinepua and Ngāi Te Ipu hold mana whenua over Whakakī Lake and associated waterways. Whakakī Lake is located 'in the East Coast of the North Island, between Wairoa and Nuhaka' (PCE, 1993b). It was once a continuous wetland system that 'extended from Opoho in the east to Waiatai Valley in the west' (Whaley et al., 2001).

Since the 1970s the local hapū had noticed significant ecological changes in the Whakakī Lake system (PCE, 1993b; Coombes & Hill, 2005) and had lobbied, unsuccessfully, for local and regional government to change flood management practices at the lake to arrest further environmental degradation and biodiversity loss. Unhappy with the (non-)response from local authorities, representatives for owners of the lake property approached the office of the PCE for assistance. The response from the Commissioner was an investigation into the management of the lagoon system.[11]

In the context of Māori environmental aspirations this letter stresses that the hapū of Whakakī strongly desire to maintain customary relationships with the lake. Such links create strong spiritual and cultural connections that give the local people 'their pride, their mana and their spiritual culture'. The bond between people and place also creates a series of obligations and responsibilities, as alluded to by the statement 'we as kai tiaki (Trustees) of the environment should endeavour to maintain all natural resources'. These relationships with whenua[12] enable the people of Whakakī to be sustained by the ancestral landscape and to continue to access their heritage.

Environmental leadership therefore is exemplified by relationships and actions that are encapsulated within the concept of kaitiakitanga. This chapter will explore a vision of leadership that is grounded in the environment, dependent on culturally appropriate relationships and manifested as kaitiakitanga.

A note on method

In this chapter I argue that kaitiakitanga is a form of environmental leadership. The letter by Huki Solomon, whakataukī and voices of kaitiaki are used to support this argument. The voices of kaitiaki were recorded as part of a doctoral project called 'Hei Whenua Papatipu' (Forster, 2012). Hei Whenua Papatipu explored contemporary kaitiakitanga with a specific focus on wetland ecosystems and the effects of laws and policy on hapū relationships with whenua.

Leadership is exhibited by a diverse range of hapū members, from kaumātua keeping alive the stories of the land, to the fishers and weavers who continue to practice customary harvesting (Forster, 2012). Another important group are those who engage with the state to ensure that Māori rights and interests are recognised within Aotearoa/New Zealand environmental policy. In this context kaitiakitanga as environmental leadership is able to achieve what Professor Sir Mason Durie (2001) refers to as the three goals of Māori development: to live as Māori, to actively participate as citizens of the world, and to enjoy good health and a high standard of living.

Hei whenua papatipu: Consolidating the base that sustains the people

In his letter, Huki Solomon emphasises the importance of the lake and associated resources, 'hei whenua papatipu' – the base that nurtures the hapū. From the multitude of fisheries and birds that were present in the past, it is clear that the lake ecosystem provided physical nourishment and contributed therefore to survival of the hapū. Mention of the activities of tūpuna, such as swimming in the river, rowing to the lake, fishing and preservation of kai, keep tūpuna constantly present in our lives. A living presence within the ancestral landscape weaves together the past, the present and future generations, creating

Whakakī Lake, Wairoa, New Zealand. Photo courtesy of the Wairoa District Council. *Graphics designed by Andre Te Hira.*

obligations and responsibilities to tūpuna and whenua. For example, the final paragraph in this letter emphasises an obligation as kaitiaki to 'maintain all natural resources' and a responsibility 'to ensure that future generations can grow up with a heritage that is a vital part of being Māori'. These obligations and responsibilities are reinforced by the bond between people and place. Solomon refers to this as 'the heritage bonds [that] give ... tangata whenua their pride, their mana and their spiritual culture'. A key function, therefore, of hapū as mana whenua is to maintain relationships with whenua and, through the practice of kaitiakitanga, protect and care for the ancestral landscape. Such activities ensure that whenua continues to nurture the hapū and remains as a cultural and spiritual base for future generations, hei whenua papatipu.

The bond between people and place is symbiotic, ' ... the rivers ... our providers, our homes, those bloodlines of Papatūānuku that will keep her living and in turn keep us living, and looking after that area' (Kaitiaki 4). Solomon described this relationship thus: 'mehemea ka ora te taonga nei, ka tū tangata ngā hapū o te Whakakī, mehemea kāore te hunga ora e manaaki, e tiaki te taonga nei, ā ka mate' (Whakakī Lake Trust, 2008). A translation is, 'if the lake is well, the mana of the hapū is maintained; if the ability to care for and protect the lake is compromised then the health and condition of the lake and the people will be diminished.' He goes on to emphatically state, 'mā tātou e manaaki, e tiaki i tēnei wā e ora ana tātou' – 'we will look after and protect it while we are alive.' This aspiration is encapsulated by the whakataukī, 'Toitū te marae a Tāne, toitū te marae a Tangaroa, toitū te iwi.' Ropata Taylor translates this as, 'When the realm of Tāne and the domains of Tangaroa are sustained, so too is the future of humanity' (Taylor, 2006, p. 3). The relationship with whenua and the health of the hapū therefore are premised on retention of the life-sustaining capacity of the ancestral landscape and Solomon clearly identifies this goal as a key obligation of hapū.

Toitūtanga: Sustainability culture

In the letter to the Commissioner, Solomon argued transformation of the environment 'due to the ecosystem being muddled with by engineers' has led to environmental degradation and loss of biodiversity:[13] 'The food source which the people of Whakaki relied on for many generations has now almost disappeared.' Despite these changes, the local hapū are still deeply rooted in and connected to this area and the associated natural resources. Remnant wetlands[14] remain highly valued ecosystems and continue to make a significant contribution to the spiritual well-being and identity of local hapū.

Environmental degradation and loss of biodiversity have however incited hapū towards actions that maintain the life-sustaining capacity of the ancestral landscape. Hapū have adapted and responded to changes that have transformed the ancestral landscape to ensure the continuance of mana whenua rights, culture and identity. This letter is but one example of that response. The letter was one of a series of protests over the state of the environment. Fortunately for the hapū of Whakakī, this letter initiated an investigation into the management of the lake, the purpose of which was to clarify responsibility for, and the extent of, the ecological decline of the Whakakī Lagoon system and to identify potential strategies for enhancement of this wetland ecosystem (PCE, 1993a, 1993b). The investigation identified both the direct role of Crown agencies in the ecological decline of Whakakī Lagoon and also the decline in hapū authority (mana whenua). It was recommended that a significant contribution from the state be made towards restoration of the lake ecosystem. An outcome of that investigation was the development of an extensive restoration and enhancement programme by Whakakī Lake Trust that began in 1996 and still continues today. Whakakī Lake Trust is responsible for the management of the lake property (Hereheretau B2L2 block). Kaitiakitanga, in particular management of tuna (eel) and wildfowl stocks, has been a core function of the Trust since it was established in 1969.

The Whakakī Lake restoration programme was the first wetland restoration programme driven and led by hapū in Aotearoa/New Zealand. The programme included collaborative working relationships with Hawke's Bay Regional Council, the Department of Conservation, the Wairoa District Council, Eastern Fish and Game, and Whakakī 2N.[15] In 1996, restoration began with major changes to the lake hydrology. After 14 months of excavation, efforts were funnelled towards a large-scale replanting programme to protect and enhance the wetland and coastal ecosystems. The programme also involves fencing and de-stocking, noxious plant and animal pest control, ecological monitoring and research related to customary harvesting, particularly of eels. Future plans exist for the development of an environmental educational programme and a native coastal bird breeding programme.[16]

The Whakakī Lake Trust hapū-based restoration programme has received both international (Ramsar) and national recognition for its work to 'restore the natural hydrology and ecology of the Whakakī Lagoon and its associated large coastal wetland system' ('Well justified' awards for top conservation efforts, 1 February 2001). The project is an exemplar of environmental leadership. Restoration and enhancement are just some activities that have emerged to maintain relationships with whenua. Restoration and enhancement enable hapū to seek new ways to strengthen connections and develop new relationships with the transformed and highly modified ancestral landscape. One kaitiaki involved in the Hei Whenua Papatipu project expressed it this way:

For me what I realised straight away is that monitoring was a chance for us to get back out on the whenua, to do it in places where we may have lost a relationship with or interaction with because of degradation or simply because people don't have time to go and gather food anymore, or the will or whatever and I see it as a really important way, just for our people to be back out there getting their hands dirty, interacting with the environment in a new way but based on traditional knowledge about what those places were for. That is the key thing to me. (Kaitiaki 13)

These types of activities serve to consolidate kaitiakitanga knowledge and practice: 'our cultural and customary knowledge of Mother Earth comes from listening and observing and nurturing her' (Kaitiaki 1). Consolidation enables hapū to fulfil customary obligations and responsibilities to tūpuna and whenua, thereby reinforcing mana whenua rights: 'It is our responsibility as kaitiaki to uphold the well-being … restoring the essence' (Kaitiaki 1). Other positive outcomes of restoration and enhancement include a strong sense of community and social cohesion:

feeling that that is where their ūkaipō is, that they have a responsibility to come back there … a responsibility to follow on from their parents, an expectation, there is an obligation that is inherent, you can't dodge it. (Kaitiaki 4)

Restoration and enhancement get people back out on the whenua and provide an opportunity for those histories layered upon the land to be passed down and in so doing facilitate the affirmation of cultural identity and well-being:

It's about pulling people back in … wanting to consolidate and bring a whole lot of people back to the context of tikanga, kawa, te reo, relationship to the marae, your own, olds, home, the whole Whakatipuranga Ruamano [Generation 2000, the Ngāti Raukawa tribal plan] sensibility. (Kaitiaki 6)

Kaitiakitanga as environmental leadership

Bishop Manuhuia Bennett once succinctly described Māori leadership along the following lines: 'Te kai a te rangatira, he kōrero, te tohu o te rangatira, he manaaki, te mahi a te rangatira, he whakatira i te iwi' (Bennett, n.d.). This whakatauākī identifies three key qualities of a leader: sound decision-making, generosity and maintaining unity.

'Te kai a te rangatira, he kōrero' emphasises that the mana of a leader is linked to their words: 'when a chief says something, that is their bond, as their mana (or honour) rests on the truth of their words.'[17] Rangatira have the ability, knowledge and wisdom to make appropriate decisions for the collective. The role of a rangatira is to listen to the people, consult with the atua and set the kaupapa and direction of a *take*. Sound decision-making is a key outcome of this process.

'Te tohu o te rangatira, he manaaki' emphasises that decision-making involves advocating for the collective and requires a rangatira to demonstrate generosity and respect.

'Te mahi a te rangatira, he whakatira i te iwi' is a reference to a key goal of tribal leadership, which is to unify the people, to create a sense of community and social cohesion and bring people together to address a kaupapa. In this context a key role of rangatira is to provide strategic leadership and direction.

Huki Solomon's vision of what constituted an appropriate relationship with whenua and his leadership, which promoted environmental sustainability, is his legacy to the hapū and future generations. His letter to the Commissioner is a narrative lamenting a lost heritage while at the same time signalling a hope for a more positive future. His words were a wero to the hapū and the state. By weaving together the past, present and future, Solomon inspired his people towards environmental action. His solution to the problem of environmental degradation and loss of biodiversity was simple. Strengthen the bond between people and place to reinforce the obligation and responsibility to care for whenua. Other kaitiaki involved in the Hei Whenua Papatipu project agreed with this solution: 'When you feel that connection to a place and feel strongly about it you will make that extra effort for it' (Kaitiaki 4). Solomon's vision was that a return to the core values of the tūpuna would enable the ancestral landscape to nurture and sustain the people, hei whenua papatipu. What emerged from this vision was a series of actions through kaitiakitanga in the form of wetland restoration and enhancement. These activities enable the people of Whakakī to achieve what Durie refers to as the key objectives of Māori development, which are to live as Māori, to participate, in this case, as environmentally responsible citizens of the world, and to enjoy good health (if the lake is well so too are the people). Although Huki Solomon is no longer with us, his vision lives on:

> Unlike other iwi, the hapū of Ngāti Hine, Ngāti Hinepua, and Ngāi Te Ipu do not have a river or awa, but make no mistake the Whakakī Lake has a similar mana to that which has been bestowed upon any river. Hence the reverence with which the homefolk both local and throughout the motu and further, hold our lake.
>
> (Whakakī Lake Trust Court Submission written by Kemp Campbell (son of Huki Solomon), 9 February 2009)

Conclusion

The efforts of our whānau (extended family) towards the restoration and enhancement of Whakakī Lake exemplify environmental leadership within a customary context. Leadership was demonstrated by our tūpuna in the way that they grounded us within a geographical space and left to us and future generations this taonga tuku iho, Whakakī Lake. Kaumātua have provided leadership by setting the direction of environmental management and through the knowledge and wisdom provided throughout the restoration and enhancement process. Kaitiaki and the community, both Māori and non-Māori, have been key players in responding to environmental crises at the lake and operationalising the hapū vision of kaitiakitanga, as 'The health and well-being of Papatūānuku is a reflection of us as people ... not just Māori people, all races' (Kaitiaki 1). The restoration and enhancement programme has brought the community together and provided us with an opportunity to continue to walk the land and engage with Papatūānuku.

Personal reflections

As an academic with an interest in the adaptation and resilience of culture, exploring the complexities of real-life experiences of our people is the key to understanding effective Māori leadership in the twenty-first century. This example of kaitiakitanga as environmental leadership from my own tūrangawaewae demonstrates that while leadership manifests in many ways, relationships and actions are fundamental to achieving hapū environmental rights and interests. There will always be a need to build capabilities and capacities. These are, however, inconsequential if we do not have confidence in the resilience of our own values, systems and people.

Acknowledgements

Tēnei te mihi mahana, te mihi aroha ki a koutou, ngā kaitiaki o te motu nei. Nā ā koutou mahi i ora te pūmanawa o te iwi kāinga nei. I would like to acknowledge the work of kaitiaki involved in the Hei Whenua Papatipu study and others working on behalf of their hapū.

REFERENCES

Bennett, Rt Rev. Manuhuia (n.d.). 'My reminiscences of the 1939 Young Māori Leaders' Conference.' Retrieved from: http://www.firstfound.org/Vol.%207New_Folder/my_reminiscences_of_the_1939_you.htm

Coombes, B. & Hill, S. (2005). *Fishing for the Land Under Water – Catchment management, wetland conservation and the Wairoa coastal lagoons.* A report prepared for the Crown Forestry Rental Trust. Auckland, New Zealand: School of Geography and Environmental Science, University of Auckland.

Durie, M.H. (2001). 'A framework for considering Māori educational advancement.' Paper prepared for Hui Taumata Mātauranga: Māori Education Summit, 23–25 February 2001, Tūrangi and Taupō.

Forster, M.E. (2012). 'Hei whenua papatipu: Kaitiakitanga and the politics of protecting the mauri of wetlands.' Unpublished PhD thesis, Te Pūtahi-a-Toi, School of Māori Studies, Massey University, Palmerston North.

Parliamentary Commissioner for the Environment (1993a). 'Investigation into the management of Whakaki Lagoon.' Wellington.

Parliamentary Commissioner for the Environment (1993b). 'Investigation into the management of Whakaki Lagoon: Background report.' Wellington.

Taylor, R. (2006, 16 September). 'Māori perspective on recreation.' Paper presented at the New Zealand Recreation Summit, Te Papa Tongarewa Museum of New Zealand, Wellington.

'"Well justified" awards for top conservation efforts.' (1 February 2001). Media Statement from Hon. Marian Hobbs, Minister of the Environment and Hon. Sandra Lee, Minister of Conservation. Retrieved September 2006 from: http://www.ramsar.org/wwd/1/wwd2001_rpt_newzealand3.htm

Whakakī Lake Trust (2008). 'Whakakī Lake management plan.'

Whaley, K.J., Clarkson, B.D., Emmett, D.K., Innes, J.G., Leathwick, J.R., Smale, M.C. & Whaley, P.T. (2001). 'Tiniroto, Waihua, Mahia and Matawai ecological districts.' Survey report for the protected natural areas programme. Department of Conservation, Gisborne.

CHAPTER 10

Kia Āio: Manaakitanga and academia

Katarina Gray-Sharp

He pātere

I begin this chapter seated at my desk on the Turitea site of Massey University (Palmerston North). Before me: a keyboard, a screen and piles of paper-bound texts. The word 'text' is family to the Latin *texere* ('to weave'). I look at my hands, ridges and muscles grown to entwine words instead of muka. To the west is where the Turitea Stream meets the Manawatū River. Every day, across these waterways, hundreds of vehicles chase one another to and from city homes.

The centre where I work is a service dedicated to supporting teaching and learning. It employs professional staff primarily, but also contains a number of academics. I have held a full-time, permanent lectureship here since November 2010. My daily tasks involve working alongside teaching staff to develop curricula, share new teaching practices and establish peer support systems. I really enjoy working with teachers and have found a niche supporting mātauranga Māori initiatives on campus. In this, I acknowledge the work of Sheeanda Field (Kaihautū Māori, Massey University Library).

My mind drifts homeward. To the northwest, the Whanganui River flows. Following her ridges north, Ruapehu and Tuhirangi come into view. Near the Kutaroa wetland, from which the Waiaruhe Stream runs to meet the Turakina River, is the marae of Raketapauma. Overlooking the wharepuni is a hill where the Old People sleep. This is the home of my Koro's childhood, and I chair a trust that administers some of the land blocks nearby. Heading south, the Opou and Mangoiwa streams are crossed, tributaries of the Hautapu and, ultimately, the Rangitīkei. Kuratahi, my home, sits on a hill south of the Opou.

Kuratahi is a marae that was established by Koro's maternal grandmother in support of the Māramatanga movement. The lands on which the marae sits belonged to her first husband's line. Although (like Koro and Dad) I lived for months at a time at Maungārongo (Ōhākune), Kuratahi is where I spent half my life. I am a trustee for my father's interests in this place. Every 27th of July, we gather here to recommit ourselves to the Māramatanga and to remember the day that Mere Rikiriki made.

Koro began farming the land – mostly dry stock – as a young teen. He taught his children and grandchildren to love Kuratahi, and served on both local and national bodies. More personally, Koro was my escort at Ngāruawahia when I debuted during the Silver Jubilee. He and Nanny met at the Hui Aranga. They were active in the Church, sending their children to Catholic boarding schools, welcoming young men from the seminary and hosting children preparing for sacrament. Like the women of Koro's line, our Nanny held authority over the marae. Raised at Taumarunui, my Rangiwēwehi-Raukawa Nanny founded her claims for obedience (and allowed openings for others to comply) on personality and hard work.

Nanny taught my tēina and me the importance of order. Nanny cleaned with newspaper, hot water, Sunlight soap and vinegar. She learnt to make korowai at Diggeress Te Kanawa's knee and was a volunteer fundraiser. She shared her skills freely and provided opportunities for them to be practised. In the year after her daughter, our Aunty and my cousins' mother, died, Nanny had me karanga by myself when we had manuhiri. Since her death, I have been joined by most of my tēina. Last year on the 27th, there were six black skirts hemmed by bare feet on snow. From Koro and Nanny, we learnt the importance of manaakitanga, and how to manaaki our manuhiri appropriately. Manaakitanga is, therefore, the first principle for my definition of leadership.

My Dad is the first of six and, like his father, a farmer. As children, Dad and Mum would take us to wānanga overseen by his Akapita, Mareikura and Tahuparae cousins. My younger brother and I spent many dawns listening to words we did not understand. Dad grew to love our Old People and they in turn taught him to appreciate the value of whakapapa. In primary school, some of our aunties and uncles suddenly became 'Cousin'. Dad would have me recite names and test me against the stones at the different urupā we visited. Whakapapa became a means of identifying my place in the world in relation to all other things around me. Whakapapa is, therefore, the second principle for my definition of leadership.

From a home of manaakitanga and whakapapa, I return to my desk to spy places close. Where the Manawatū River meets the sea, the dunes lead south to Waitārere and the sands of Hōkio. Following her stream east, towards Lake Horowhenua, Ngātokowaru is seen. Nearby, my Nanny was brought up by her kuia in a blue mud hut, and I am a trustee for a land block here. Returning to the Manawatū, the Ōroua tributary can be followed upstream where it flows in the shadow of Whakaari. At Rongopai, where bones lie, the Ōroua can be followed northeast to Aorangi, or crossed to Kai Iwi. Koro's photograph hangs on a Kauwhata wall. I attend meetings here for these, the places of my mother's childhood.

Koro served in D Company (having lied about his age), and worked as a cook and truck driver after some years with the Department of Māori Affairs. He loved to sing, and travelled regularly to act as the Master of Ceremonies for celebrations across the motu. His sister, Nanny Kawa, used to run noho marae at Kai Iwi for the mokopuna and their mothers. A natural extension of (the Hui Aranga club) St Paul's, she taught us girls to hope Tainui-style, which got me into a bit of trouble when we joined Ruapehu in 1983. I learnt to plait poi and to not chatter (too much), but the best part was playing/fighting with all the cousins. As a result of the noho (but mostly because another one of our nannies, Nanny Pearl, told me to), my karanga at Aorangi happened before my karanga at Kuratahi.

My Nanny attended St Joseph's Māori Girls' School for one week before returning to bury her kuia. Instead of going back to school, she helped raise money for the war effort and got a job. Once married, she volunteered, and worked in factories and at St Dominic's School for the Deaf. Nanny was direct, had a huge laugh and gave really good advice. After she became a bilateral amputee in her sixties, we spent most days together roaming in my car.

Nanny and Koro used housies, card games and raffles to fundraise for the Māori Battalion Hall, St Paul's and Caccia Birch (among others). My first real job was at a midweek housie while living with them in 1989. We spent weekends collecting watercress and kawakawa, and cheating at cards. From Koro and Nanny, we learnt how aroha can be music and laughter and giving without loss. Aroha is, therefore, the third principle for my definition of leadership.

My Mum is the third of nine. Her maternal line is matekite, Nanny's mother hosting a monthly rā for people to discuss matters wairua. Mum learnt to blend Nanny's and the Māramatanga's teachings, giving us water and words for those we love. My brother and I would play (or fight not-so-secretly) while she talked kaitiaki with the nannies, her siblings, or Dad's cousins. We came to understand how easy it is to believe in something others say is untrue when you are shown where to find it. That is why wairua is my fourth principle of leadership.

Manaakitanga, whakapapa, aroha and wairua. There is a permanence in these words, their power, their places. I return via the Manawatū to my desk and a screen full of text. There is finishing to do.

I am the second of three and an only daughter. There is a big picture in my parents' living room of me, aged two, riding my four-year-old brother's back. Although a few photos of our baby brother and me are pinned to the wall, most fill albums Dad stores in an old filing cabinet in his office. I remember crawling into my brothers' beds as a child, feeling settled by their closeness and the nests we made.

Mum's brother and Dad were schoolmates, which is how my parents met. A decade later, Uncle came to Kuratahi for a weekend and never left, making the area home. He cared for my younger brother and me while Mum and Dad travelled doing land claims research. Having cooked with Koro, Uncle found a place in the kitchens of his brother-in-law's people. He taught us how to chop vegetables for chow mein, to make wontons and to clean up as you go.

Our eldest brother has been confined to a wheelchair since 1979. During the worst years, my tuakana received prayers from people all over the world. Our grandparents travelled to him and became a group of four. They would spend summers together and worked on stalls at the College gala day, Mum's dad on the coconut shy and Dad's mum on the frybread. Their albums, full of big hair and large prints, share photographs of hot days at Waitārere Beach. To the west, beyond the pictures' edge, the Whanganui, Turakina, Rangitīkei, Hōkio and Manawatū mingle in waves.

And here I end and bind.

An essay

Academia is an emerging social institution, honed by the literate cultures within which it operates. Its European development can be discussed in terms of the chronicles of Western civilisation. These chronicles can be divided into four eras: ancient, 'Christianism, nationalism, and economism' (Ford, 2002, p. 20).

Like other 'complex social forms that reproduce themselves', academia is a social institution (Miller, 2011, para. 1). As an emerging entity, it is 'a space/time in which being together on the terms of thought-in-relation can be held open as a question' (Simon, 2001, p. 53). Academia offers hierarchical arrangements for certifying those who do and do not belong. Membership is extended to those able 'to invent the university by mimicking its language while finding some idiosyncrasy, a personal history ... and the requirements of convention, the history of discipline' (Bartholomae, 1985, p. 135).

For the Ancient era, academia emphasises a Greek heritage. Although the templar *per-ankh* of Ancient Eygpt (c. 2000 BC) were arguably the first examples of formal higher education (Lulat, 2005, p. 46), Pythagoras is acknowledged as the originator of the Greek institution (Holton, 1995). Specialist slaves, *paidagogos*,[18] taught the male children of Greece. Gymnasia, like Plato's (c. 387–84 BC), offered instruction to older citizens. Horace (Epistles II, 2, 45) would later describe the sacred grove leading to Plato's school as *silvas academi*, reflecting the hero Akademos for whom the site was named and providing an etymology for what is now termed 'academia'. Such an etymology is fitting, perhaps, given that Plato and his student, Aristotle, are identified as the source of the 'post-alphabetic' society (Havelock, 1980, p. 96).

Literacy is from *litera* meaning 'letter of the alphabet', its Greek conception descending from Mesopotamian cuneiform and Egyptian hieroglyphs through Cretan and West Semitic[19] writing systems (Powell, 2010; see also Havelock, 1980). The 'adaptation' facilitated the 'abstraction' and subsequent 'recognition (the original Greek work [sic] for 'reading')' of symbols to sounds, allowing for the 'possibility of a popular literacy' (Havelock, 1980, pp. 93–94). The advent of the Roman Empire saw Greek become a subject, as well as a language, of instruction. Thus, Greek language and literature were maintained via Roman adoption up to the 'seventh century A.D., when the study of Greek finally had come to an end in Latin Europe' (Goitein & Stillman, 2010, p. 56).

After 476 AD, the church became the European home of higher education, initiating the period of Christianism. The earliest universities were learning guilds chartered by imperial or papal authority to allow conferment of degrees. They undertook advanced teaching of students in areas such as arts, medicine, law and theology (Patterson, 1997). The institution was incubated in the humanism of the Renaissance period, becoming a site for rhetorically exploring the literary 'legacy of antiquity' through 'the rediscovery and study of ancient Greek and Roman texts' (Mann, 1996, p. 2).

La Sorbonne, France's oldest establishment, was influential in transmitting the humanist position. It achieved state patronage from the thirteenth century, initiating the concept of the academy as a public institution. Teaching was conducted in specialised divisions, separate from science research units, in a system that was 'highly centralized and bureaucratic' (Anderson, 2006, p. 30). Although a theological institution, the library contained the 'common school texts [such] as Cato', in addition to the 'Latin Aristotle' and 'Plato in Latin dress' (Ullman, 1973, p. 43). The university's Fichet and de la Pierre introduced the first printing press to Paris in 1462 (Humphreys, 1868). Fichet's printing outputs reflected 'his humanistic interests'; Cicero's *De Officiis*, an engagement with the work of the Stoic philosopher Panaetius of Rhodes, appears (Nauert, 1995, p. 119). During the Enlightenment, La Sorbonne was to provide housing for some of the period's *philosophes*, such as Diderot (Bristow, 2011, para. 2).

The Enlightenment signalled the advent of secularity and expansion in the period of nationalism. From the Scientific Revolution's initiation in the sixteenth century via Copernicus and Vesalius through to the French Revolution, the Enlightenment is 'characterized by dramatic revolutions in science, philosophy, society and politics' (Bristow, 2011, para. 1). Luminaries of the period include Thomas Hobbes (English empiricist), René Descartes (French rationalist), John Locke (English empiricist), Isaac Newton (English scientist), Adam Smith (Scottish economist) and Immanuel Kant (German philosopher). By the 1700s, presses had appeared throughout the Northern Hemisphere and 170 universities had been established throughout Europe. The model of the modern university was not far away.

In 1810, Wilhelm von Humboldt, J.G. Fichte, and Friedrich Schleiermacher helped establish the model modern university (Anderson, 2006). Initially called Universität zu Berlin (University of Berlin), the institution was renamed Humboldt-Universität zu Berlin in 1949. The Humboldtian model offered a publicly funded institution, which taught the traditional humanities curriculum in one body and offered the doctoral degree. Thus, the principle of *Lehrfreiheit* (freedom of teaching) allowed appointments by the state, with the community of academics retaining the right to determine the criteria (for example, qualifications, publications, professional memberships). Although privileging of international study by teaching staff began much earlier,[20] the availability of the doctoral degree enticed students from as far as the United States (Anderson, 2006). Further, the model built on the idea, begun at the university in Göttingen, of professors as producers of original research. Research-trained learners worked alongside these teachers in *Wissenschaft*: 'the objective and critical pursuit of science and learning and the establishment of truth through rigorous academic methods' (Anderson, 2006, p. 29).

Comparatively, Oxford, 'the oldest university in the English-speaking world' (University of Oxford, 2009, para. 1), was a gradual meeting of the religious[21] and the social elite.[22] Adoption of research training at the University of Oxford was slow, but accelerated after the Humboldtian model was adopted by Yale in 1861. Alongside Cambridge, Edinburgh and London, Oxford began offering higher doctoral degrees in the 1870s. In 1917, Oxford introduced the Doctor of Philosophy, and a British union of teaching and research was finally comprehended.

Arguments for state support of British universities began in the nineteenth century. In 1836, the British Parliament proposed 'both that state sanction was necessary to confer degrees, and that university education could be detached from religion' (Anderson, 2006, p. 28). This was done via the charter to establish the University of London as 'a public, non-denominational body which did not teach but administered examinations and degrees for "affiliated" colleges' (Anderson, 2006, p. 27). The idea was to see replication in New Zealand.

In 1870, amid extensive politicking, the University of New Zealand was enacted ('Education', 1966). As the numbers of provincial institutions rose, the University of New Zealand became the body of examination, measuring and therefore controlling entrance to the academic elite. From 1922 the examination role was devolved and in 1947 the provincial call for institutional autonomy began to gain ground. By the end of 1961, New Zealand had a developed, multi-unit tertiary system. The post-Bretton Woods period of economism (or 'international capitalism' – Ford, 2002, p. 31) and subsequent massification had arrived.

Massification is mass production and consumption, in this case, of higher education. It is a phenomenon associated with high levels of demand, increased participation (domestic and international), and growing diversity among producers and consumers. Higher education expansion patterns have been, in both developed and developing countries, 'remarkably similar, consistent and accelerating growth' (Scott, 2010, p. 218). Thus, massification has resulted in 'the assimilation of postsecondary education into the ordinary life of the society' (Trow, 2000, p. 7).

From 1988, higher education in New Zealand began to change rapidly. A working group, created as part of wider social reform, offered rebranding – Post-Compulsory Education and Training – and an economic role (Hawke, 1988). Institutional competition helped construct students as consumers; 'universities were less commonly seen as elite institutions, but rather as mass educators' (Larner & Le Heron, 2005, p. 849). Echoing 'corporate managerialism', universities began projects of 'transparent alignment', introduced 'user-charges', and promoted 'the transformation of higher education in New Zealand from universal welfare entitlement into private investment in "human capital"' (Peters, 1997, p. 16). What is (still) a public good in parts of Europe was positioned here as a private one.

The primary social benefit identified with market models of higher education is increased equality through expanded participation (Strathdee, 2004). The 1992 enactment of the student loan scheme had definite participatory outcomes. Student headcounts doubled between 1994 and 2008 (Ministry of Education, 2009) with Māori participation peaking at 23.1 per cent in 2004 (Ministry of Education, 2011a). By 2010, university enrolments had grown to 179,013, with Māoridom contributing 15,335 (Ministry of Education, 2011b). Unfortunately, this expanded participation has not seen increased equality.

According to the Organisation for Economic Co-operation and Development (2011), New Zealand's income inequality has been above the mean since 1990. Perry (2012) defined 35 per cent of single adult households in 2011 as income impoverished. Between 170,000 and 270,000 children were living in poverty. Of those children, 47 per cent were from Māori or Pasifika families. Furthermore, 'continuing manifestations of discrimination' against Māori include 'unequal access to services' (Committee on the Rights of the Child, 2011, p. 5). As inequalities persist, commitment to the market model appears more political than evidence-based.

I argue that the contemporary administration of academia is ideologically driven. Though resources were no doubt important in Ancient Greece, Christian France and the nationalistic University of New Zealand, the current turn is troubling. Higher education trends towards internationalisation as a means to fund institutions and grow domestic capacity. Internationalisation, unfortunately, is mired in the inconveniences of global economies; when the markets are in crisis, incomes decrease. Further, the practice reinforces the shift of responsibility for higher education away from the nation-state. In the shadow of economism, ideals of public education are rendered quiet.

A reflection

In choosing to write this chapter, I was asked to consider what constitutes Māori leadership in academia. In order to do so, I began with two narratives. The first located me to identify some principles of Māori leadership. The second discussed academia to identify the space within which the principles might operate. The intention of this third section is to reflectively apply one of those principles to that space.

Four principles of Māori leadership appeared in the first narrative. Manaakitanga focuses on standards and hospitality. Whakapapa locates me as the speaker and identifies my relationships with all other things. Aroha offers hope-filled connection and giving without cost. Wairua is the potential of the unseen. By blending my upbringing and what I have learnt, I understand that each principle can operate differently in academia. This narrative focuses on the first principle, manaakitanga.

At home, manaakitanga is a first principle when dealing with strangers. Among my father's people, we talk of the negotiations used to ensure safety when two groups first meet. The processes throughout the marae, from the paepae to stores, impart our rules of engagement. Interactions and representation are controlled by the home people. Newcomers are welcome to learn our ways by working alongside us clearing tables, washing dishes or preparing vegetables.

Those who are trusted may have an opportunity to represent us in engagements with others who come. In this way, the Stranger is offered an opportunity to rest from their wandering (Gudykunst, 1983).

Manaakitanga as a leadership principle involves standards and hospitality. Although other views of 'standard' are possible, I cite D. Royce Sadler (1987) in deference to my new discipline:

> a definite level of excellence or attainment, or a definite degree of any quality viewed as a prescribed object of endeavour or as the recognized measure of what is adequate for some purpose, so established by authority, custom, or consensus. (p. 194)

As noted in my previous work, I think of hospitality as conditional (Gray-Sharp, 2011). Ingrid M. Hoofd (2011, p. 63), a teacher of ethics at the National University of Singapore, talks about how 'hospitable communication … always simultaneously involves a commanding and the withdrawal of command'. Fed by the practices of Home, hospitality becomes the tides of negotiated connection.

The standards and hospitality of manaakitanga have appeared in my academic life in a number of ways. Standards emerged as a theme right at the beginning when I was employed in my first teaching position while still an undergraduate in 1997. Like many others founded after the Education Amendment Act 1990, the Private Training Establishment where I worked provided vocational training (in this case, for would-be chefs). My job was to develop and teach a curriculum to a group of learners, most of whom had recently left school with few literacy or numeracy skills. To cope, I managed my teaching like I managed my learning: through clear goals and structured communication. This meant my standards and their teaching were able to reflect our learners and the skills they were aiming to achieve.

Hospitality, in my case, includes developing systems for peer support. As an undergraduate, I was active in the Māori student network, planning, organising and coordinating alongside my mates. I began e-teaching in 2001, establishing my social media practice while tutoring. This evolved into a course management system-based community in 2006, m-learning research outputs and Tweeps. In 2012, a number of other peer-based projects drew me. Tīwaha offers a weekly immersion environment for reo speakers from beginners to fluent. My role has included administering meetings, promotion (press releases, event notifications) and social media (developing Twitter and Facebook profiles). A second group has shown interest in reigniting Te Matawhānui on campus. Te Matawhānui was the national 'Māori University Teachers Association' originally established in 1989 (Victoria University of Wellington, 1990, p. 9). At the time of writing, my role involves developing an organisational profile by emailing Māori staff a semi-regular factsheet on Te Matawhānui's history. All of this work is done to offer a space within which people can negotiate relationships.

In academic leadership, standards offer goals and the means to measure them, while hospitality provides spaces for achieving them. However, academia is more explicit about standards than hospitality. All New Zealand universities must meet certain standards in order to qualify for funding. For example, in order to be eligible for state support, qualifications must meet the standards established by the Committee on University Academic Programmes (New Zealand Academic Audit Unit, 2011). Although our universities intend for their qualifications to be completed by learners, there is insufficient conformity to this norm. In 2010, the overall qualification completion rate for universities was 67 per cent (Tertiary Education Commission, 2010). The completion rate for Māori learners was 55 per cent. It may be necessary for the system to make hospitality a more explicit aspect.

I aim to make hospitality more explicit in my teaching environments. The development of the content and form of this chapter has contributed to that process. The content has articulated new aspects of my teaching philosophy, helping me better meet my responsibilities as I locate myself in the academic space. The form is offered as a means of describing the negotiation between a Māori identity (pātere), academic acculturation (essay and citations) and an ever-present alterity (reflection).

I acknowledge you, my tuakana, and finish here.

E tau nei te aroha o te iwi e ... i.

REFERENCES

Anderson, R. (2006). *British Universities Past and Present.* London: Hambledon Continuum.

Bano, M. (2012). *The Rational Believer: Choices and decisions in the madrasas of Pakistan.* New York: Cornell University.

Bartholomae, D. (1985). 'Inventing the university.' In M. Rose (ed.), *When a Writer Can't Write: Studies in writer's block and other composing-process problems* (pp. 134–65). New York, NY: Guilford Press. Retrieved from: http://www.utoronto.ca/writing/Dec2010/Bartholomae.pdf

Bolton, P. (2012). 'Oxford "elitism"' (SN/SG/616). Retrieved from: http://www.parliament.uk/briefing-papers/SN00616

Bristow, W. (2011). 'Enlightenment.' In E.N. Zalta (ed.), *The Stanford Encyclopedia of Philosophy* (Summer edn). Retrieved from: http://plato.stanford.edu/archives/sum2011/entries/enlightenment/

Committee on the Rights of the Child (2011). 'Fifty-sixth session – Concluding observations: New Zealand.' Retrieved from: http://www2.ohchr.org/english/bodies/crc/crcs56.htm

'Education', 'university – University of New Zealand'. (1966). In A.H. McLintock (ed.), *An Encyclopaedia of New Zealand*. Retrieved from: http://www.teara.govt.nz/en/1966/e

Ford, M.P. (2002). *Beyond the Modern University: Toward a constructive postmodern university.* Westport, CT: Praeger.

Goitein, S.D. & Stillman, N.A. (2010). *Studies in Islamic History and Institutions.* Leiden, The Netherlands: Koninklijke Brill NV.

Gray-Sharp, K. (2011). 'Ō rātou kāinga: Tino rangatiratanga and contemporary housing policy.' In V.M.H. Tawhai & K. Gray-Sharp (eds), *'Always Speaking': The Treaty of Waitangi and public policy* (pp. 191–212). Wellington, New Zealand: Huia.

Gudykunst, W.B. (1983). 'Toward a typology of stranger-host relationships.' *International Journal of Intercultural Relations, 7*(4), 401–13. doi: 10.1016/0147-1767(83)90046-9.

Havelock, E.A. (1980). 'The coming of literate communication to Western culture.' *Journal of Communication, 30*(1), 90–98.

Hawke, G.R. (1988). *Report on Postcompulsory Education and Training in New Zealand.* Wellington, New Zealand: Office of the Associate Minister of Education.

Holton, S.A. (1995). 'It's nothing new! A history of conflict in higher education.' *New Directions for Higher Education, 92,* 11–18.

Hoofd, I.M. (2011). 'Questioning (as) violence: Teaching ethics in a global knowledge enterprise.' *Ethics and Education, 6*(1), 53–67.

Humphreys, H.N. (1868). *A History of the Art of Printing from its Invention to its Widespread Development in the Middle of the Sixteenth Century.* London, UK: Bernard Quaritch. Retrieved from: http://books.google.co.nz/books?id=lHgWAQAAMAAJ&source=g bs_navlinks_s

Larner, W. & Le Heron, R. (2005). 'Neo-liberalizing spaces and subjectivities: Reinventing New Zealand universities.' *Organization, 12*(6), 843–62.

Lulat, Y.G.-M. (2005). *A History of African Higher Education from Antiquity to the Present: A critical synthesis.* Westport, CT: Praeger.

Mann, N. (1996). 'The origins of humanism.' In J. Kraye (ed.), *The Cambridge Companion to Renaissance Humanism* (pp. 1–19). Cambridge, UK: Cambridge University Press.

Miller, S. (2001). 'Social institutions.' In E.N. Zalta (ed.), *The Stanford Encyclopedia of Philosophy* (Summer edn). Retrieved from: http://plato.stanford.edu/archives/spr2011/entries/social-institutions/

Ministry of Education (2009). 'Student loan scheme annual report to 30 June 2009.' Retrieved from: http://www.educationcounts.govt.nz/publications/series/2555/58406/2

Ministry of Education (2011a). 'Participation rates.' Excel Workbook. Retrieved from: http://www.educationcounts.govt.nz/statistics/tertiary_education/participation

Ministry of Education (2011b). 'Provider-based enrolments.' Excel Workbook. Retrieved from: http://www.educationcounts.govt.nz/statistics/tertiary_education/participation

Nauert, C.G. (1995). *Humanism and the Culture of Renaissance Europe.* Cambridge, UK: Cambridge University Press.

New Zealand Academic Audit Unit (2011). 'Academic quality assurance of New Zealand universities.' Retrieved from: http://www.nzuaau.ac.nz/qapublication

Organisation for Economic Co-operation and Development (2011). Country note: New Zealand. In *Divided We Stand: Why inequality keeps rising*. Paris, France: Organisation for Economic Co-operation and Development. Retrieved from: http://www.oecd.org/els/socialpoliciesanddata/dividedwestandwhyinequalitykeepsrising.htm

Patterson, G. (1997). *The University from Ancient Greece to the 20th Century*. Palmerston North, New Zealand: Dunmore Press.

Perry, B. (2012). *Household Incomes in New Zealand: Trends in indicators of inequality and hardship 1982 to 2011*. Wellington, New Zealand: Ministry of Social Development. Retrieved from: http://www.msd.govt.nz/about-msd-and-our-work/publications-resources/monitoring/household-incomes/index.html

Peters, M. (1997). 'Introduction: The university in crisis.' In M. Peters (ed.), *Cultural Politics and the University in Aotearoa/New Zealand* (pp. 15–50). Palmerston North, New Zealand: Dunmore Press.

Powell, B.B. (2010). 'Alphabet and writing.' In M. Gagarin (ed.), *The Oxford Encyclopedia of Ancient Greece and Rome* (vol. 1, pp. 76–80). New York, NY: Oxford University Press.

Sadler, D.R. (1987). 'Specifying and promulgating achievement standards.' *Oxford Review of Education*, *13*(2), 191–209.

Salter, H.E., & Lobel, M.D. (eds). (1954). *The University of Oxford. A History of the County of Oxford* (vol. 3, pp. 1–38). Retrieved from: http://www.british-history.ac.uk/report.aspx?compid=63862

Scott, P. (2010). 'Higher education: An overview.' In P. Peterson, E. Baker & B. McGaw (eds), *International Encyclopedia of Education* (3rd ed., pp. 217–28). Elsevier. doi: 10.1016/B978-0-08-044894-7.00820-4.

Simon, R.I. (2001). 'The university: A place to think?' In H.A. Giroux & K. Myrsiades (eds), *Beyond the Corporate University: Culture and pedagogy in the new millennium* (pp. 45–56). Lanham, MD: Rowman & Littlefield.

Strathdee, R. (2003). 'The "third way" and vocational education and training in New Zealand.' *Journal of Educational Enquiry*, *4*(1), 31–48.

Tertiary Education Commission (2010). 'About universities.' Retrieved from: http://www.tec.govt.nz/Learners-Organisations/Learners/performance-in-tertiary-education/performance-by-type-of-tertiary-provider/about-universities

Trow, M. (2000). *From Mass Higher Education to Universal Access: The American advantage* [CSHE.1.00]. Retrieved from: http://cshe.berkeley.edu/publications/publications.php?a=16

Ullman, B.L. (1973). *Studies of the Italian Renaissance* (2nd edn). Rome, Italy: Storia e Letteratura.

University of Oxford (2009). 'A brief history of the University.' Retrieved from: http://www.ox.ac.uk/about_the_university/introducing_oxford/a_brief_history_of_the_university/index.html

Victoria University of Wellington (1990). 'Report on te hui-ā-tau ā Te Matawhānui.' Te Tira Whakaemi Kōrero, Department of Māori Studies. Retrieved from: http://www.trc.org.nz/content/report-te-hui-tau-te-matawhanui

CHAPTER **11**

Art Education: A portal to the knowledge of two worlds

Piki Diamond

Introduction

During my years at college I dreamed of becoming a secondary school art teacher; it seemed a valid occupation to incorporate what I loved doing. At the age of 17, I could never have conceived that I would be researching art education pedagogies, epistemologies and investigating possible ways on how Māori world views, ideals and pedagogies could be integrated with technology to improve the learning opportunities and knowledge development of students.

The eldest twin, and one of six children, I am of Ngāti Tūwharetoa and Ngā Pūhi descent, though born and raised in Tauranga with our adoptive iwi Ngāti Ranginui, Ngāi Te Rangi and Ngāti Pūkenga ki Tauranga. Growing up around the local marae, Te Ao Māori was centralised and normal. This way of being was much more organic and natural to my identity as Māori. There is no question that when I entered the academy I had to learn to navigate the daily institutional processes and procedures with my own identity as Māori, which initially was very challenging.

This chapter will highlight a number of personal as well as professional experiences influencing my decision to pursue an academic career. Many of my experiences draw on my journey as both an undergraduate and postgraduate student. The importance of having an institution support network and the desire to make a contribution to my communities were perhaps the most significant factors in my academic development leading to a career in academia. However, I have experienced a number of systemic and institutional challenges that do disrupt the ability of Māori to realise their full potential in academic settings and these will be discussed. In sharing my journey, I hope to provide food for thought on ways other Māori scholars interested in pursuing a career in academia can be equally successful.

Driven by experiences

In the third year of my Bachelor of Visual Arts degree my dream of becoming a secondary school art teacher was fraught with a number of personal challenges. Despite the numerous detours I have taken, I have found myself more on the road to becoming an academic in higher education and wanting to explore creativity in a much wider academic context. This change in career pathway came about during my third year in the Bachelor of Visual Arts.

After experiencing the first critique in my third year I realised I needed to seek further advice and knowledge from a Māori visual arts lecturer. Why? Because it became very clear to me, when critiquing the arts, that how I engaged with artworks, with taonga and mahi toi was very different to my non-Māori peers and lecturers. I did not know how or why it was different – all I knew was that it was different and that it had something to do with my cultural world view. Similarly, the majority of my lecturers were non-Māori and most of my learning about the visual arts was from within the dominant mainstream paradigm, and based on gallery-valued dogma and the conceptual knowledge formed within the mainstream paradigm.

In my search for a Māori arts lecturer who was culturally aware of my situation, I had the very good fortune of meeting Chaz Doherty (of Ngāi Tūhoe and Ngā Puhi descent), a master's student and lecturer in the Certificate of Art and Design Intermediate (CADI) programme at Auckland University of Technology (AUT). Over time Doherty became my mentor and good friend. His studio space became my classroom; a space for discussions about Te Ao Māori and how my art practice is innately connected to, and an expression of, who I am, as well as Te Ao Māori. For the first time since leaving Tauranga 14 years prior, I was able to find a connection to my Māori heritage.

It was at this stage that I realised how Eurocentric the visual arts curriculum and assessment criteria were, and how these systems often constrained Māori and other Indigenous students from engaging in visual arts from their own Indigenous perspectives. Elected by my peers, I became a student representative and often students came to me upset by their interactions with lecturers. A number of these cases were in regards to cultural insensitivity, due to what I later came to recognise as cultural ignorance. This planted the seed for my wanting to instigate change for our Māori and Pasifika students. With guidance from Doherty and after some time away from university I found the energy to contemplate the importance of beginning a new career in academia.

My plan to study a master's in the visual arts was quickly redirected once the visual arts selection panel interviewed me. My wanting to investigate how Māori engage with taonga and the learning that comes from that process did not fit into the assessment criteria for the degree – yet another cultural barrier in mainstream visual arts programmes. Thankfully, they were knowledgeable enough to connect me to the Māori department, Te Ara Poutama, who ran the Master of Arts in Māori Development programme, and where my acceptance into the programme effectively launched my career in academia back in March 2009.

Fortunately, the start of my master's programme coincided with a new scholarship programme, called the Hāpai (to lift up) programme. The programme was initiated by the Māori Advancement Office and funded by the university's Equity Office. Designed and facilitated by Maxine Graham (Māori advancement coordinator), the purpose of this scholarship was to give fledgling postgraduate students the opportunity to work alongside academics within their chosen discipline. A main goal of the programme was to increase the number of Māori academics within the institute and to plan for the succession of other current Māori academic staff. Though this programme was funded by the Equity Office, it was envisaged that eventually it would be adopted and managed by all the faculties of the university.

Through the relationship I had built with the staff in CADI, and with Doherty about to leave, I was initiated into the CADI programme as Kaihāpai (Supporter) and assigned a tutor role, engaging with students based in the studios at Awataha, on Auckland's North Shore. These students were mainly of Māori and/or Pasifika descent. The Hāpai programme also funded my studies to do the Certificate in Tertiary Teaching, which I successfully completed that year.

As a full-time student, I spent most of my time in Ngā Pia, the postgraduate room of Te Ara Poutama. I also became involved in the monthly wānanga and writing retreats that gave Māori and Pasifika students across the university the opportunity to meet and share knowledge and experiences. After successfully completing my first year, I became more confident to take on more responsibilities with CADI, and within the Māori and Pasifika student community.

In addition to working with the Awataha students, I was asked by CADI to design a painting workshop that integrated Māori views and concepts of art. The Pro-Vice-Chancellor Māori, Associate Professor Pare Keiha, also invited me to participate in the Manu Ao Academy. The three objectives of the Manu Ao Academy were: 'Accelerating Māori leadership, Strengthening the links between Māori Academics and Māori Professionals and Advancing Māori scholarship' (Manu Ao, 2010). The wānanga brought together Māori academic representatives from the eight universities in Aotearoa/New Zealand to discuss the various dimensions of the academy, to consider ways in which Māori can thrive within the academy, and to explore different kinds of leadership to support new and emerging Māori academics working in the academy. The wānanga provided a space for these topics and problems to be discussed and possible solutions found. Guest speakers at the wānanga provided guidance and inspiration to continue building Māori success in the academy. Away from the wānanga this culture was being supported by weekly seminars and motivational emails from leading Māori academics, community and business leaders.

The Manu Ao Academy network opened my eyes to a range of different possibilities and opportunities. Unfortunately, when the time came for me to look for full-time employment, the School of Art & Design at AUT had no full-time positions available. However, due to my participation and contribution back into the university I was offered a split contract between Art & Design and Te Ara Poutama. This offer was presented at the same time that I was offered a new Māori student advisory position at Massey University. I took the latter opportunity with Massey, looking forward to the new environment and meeting new people.

Working in different institutions not only gave me an opportunity to network and get to know other academics and staff within the tertiary sector, it also provided a wider understanding of the sector and how different institutions view each other. My role with Massey University was as a Te Rau Whakaara (TRW) Māori Student Advisor. Professor Sir Mason Durie conceived the strategy that underpinned TRW. The position required me to put in place a number of systems, tools and resources that aided in the recruitment and retention of Māori students to Massey University. Durie adapted the holistic well-being model of Te Whare Tapa Whā to supporting students at university. TRW embraced Durie's guiding principles of whakapiri (engagement), whakamana (empowerment) and whakamārama (enlightenment). We then worked with Māori communications manager Nick Maaka and added another principle, whānau (family). This encompassed the ethos of TRW and created the identity 'wh4nau'. My whole experience with Massey not only introduced me to other passionate Māori people within academia; it also highlighted the complexities of working within an often top-down bureaucratic system.

During my time with Massey University, Associate Professor Pare Keiha and Professor Tania Ka'ai of AUT continued to keep in contact with me, often expressing their desire to see me return to AUT. That opportunity came in the form of an academic role, designed for a new academic who had an interest in pedagogies, education and technology. These were all areas I am deeply passionate about and in which I was progressing as part of my master's research. I was successful in attaining the position of Learning & Teaching Consultant, based in AUT's Centre for Learning & Teaching. My experiences from my art practices through to my master's studies have been the driving force that guides my research and career endeavours. It is through qualifying these experiences with theories that I may be better informed to contribute to positive development for future Māori students and their communities.

Driven by theory

My master's thesis was driven by my own personal experiences within the bachelor's degree and as a mature-aged Māori student. I had observed while completing my Bachelor's degree the tendency of lecturers to overcomplicate simple ideas, the dislocation of the theories being taught and discussed from the students' reality and a disregard of the importance or the role of emotional receptivity when critiquing art works. This seemed evident to me, especially as I was trying to make sense of their teaching from my Māori world view.

Given that the majority of Māori students within Aotearoa/New Zealand are continuing to enrol in mainstream universities and polytechnics (Ministry of Education, 2011), there appears to be a need to ensure that Te Ao Māori is better represented, acknowledged and valued in the Aotearoa/New Zealand curriculum and academia. Another challenge exists whereby the ratio and capacity of Māori academics within faculties and departments are disproportionately lower than non-Māori academics. This deficiency can place unrealistic demands on Māori academics to instigate change within existing mainstream curriculum and pedagogy, to be inclusive of Te Ao Mārama (i.e. Māori ways of knowing and understanding the world) while at the same time trying to balance their commitments to teaching, research, family and other hapū and iwi commitments. The current monocultural or industrialist perspective of the mainstream curriculum poses a political and philosophical challenge that hinders the advancement of Māori students.

My thesis investigates how the philosophical barriers could be overcome. The thesis describes the influences that have shaped the current visual arts curriculum and then identifies Māori concepts, practices and social structures that influence and are influenced by visual arts practices. The thesis identifies the similarities between Te Ao Māori and movements and philosophies that have developed during the industrialist mainstream education era. Theories associated with a holistic approach to education had the strongest similarities with Te Ao Māori. Gallegos Nava's (2012) matrix illustrates how combined Western theorists can provide the systematic thinking that underpins holistic education. When I was working on designing a bicultural model I noted that creation perceived from a Māori design perspective – the takarangi (double spiral) – and that of Western science – the DNA strand (double helix) – was identical.

Dubberly Design Office's (2010) Creative Process also illustrates these similarities and shows how the process does not change, only the terminology and context. For example, the Creative Process consists of the stages, Observe, Reflect, then Make. Scientific process is to observe, hypothesise then experiment. Observing is the act of objectively collecting data and information. Reflecting and hypothesising is the synthesising of the data until such a point where the idea can be manifested, to be made or experimented.

Though the holistic approach to education is more aligned to Te Ao Māori, it is not exclusive to Māori. Promoting holistic education to become the pedagogy at the centre of Aotearoa/New Zealand's education system not only avoids the political anxiety that promoting an overtly Māori pedagogy might provoke, but would also reestablish the student at the centre of education.

This comes at the time when the Industrial Age is being transcended by the Information Age, with analogue technology becoming obsolete and digital technology in the ascendancy. Data and information is stored in the Cloud, accessed by pocket-sized devices and constantly at people's fingertips. So here we see the Industrial education system being turned upside down. Educational history has often seen subjective disciplines, such as the arts and social sciences, at the bottom of the hierarchy, whereas objective quantitative disciplines such as mathematics and science have reigned supreme. However, in the Information Age, business, society, universities and governments are calling for innovation, which is the fusion of creativity and science, and when these are joined with business it becomes an entrepreneurial venture.

The skill sets utilised in the arts are now the very skills required to bring new and productive ideas and products to fruition. These skill sets include training in observation, deciphering visual codes and/or symbols, critiquing and analysing, experimentation, storytelling, composition, visual aesthetic design, self-motivation, self-direction, time management and most importantly, creativity. The general public and non-art communities often overlook these skills, as many only see and place value on the final artifact, which the artist or art student produces. The medium and/or vocation to be an artist is chosen, as this is how the artistic person observes, deciphers, engages and reflects on what is happening in the world around them, how it impacts upon and influences them. Their creations, what they choose to contribute to their world, are sourced from those experiences.

The misunderstanding of the value and role of art education has come from the Industrial-derived education system. However, if you refer to the artist within the traditional Māori context, for example, the tohunga whakairo, they were highly regarded within their communities. This may also be due to the fact that the tohunga whakairo did not create artifacts; they created implements, buildings, clothing and many other items that were required. In today's context the tohunga whakairo would be a designer and their schooling would be categorised to their chosen discipline: fashion, architecture, product and so forth. However, like the tohunga whakairo, the artistic person does not confine their creativity to the silo of one discipline. The creative person seeks something new, and in order to do so, needs to have a multitude of experiences.

Steve Jobs articulated the necessity to have various experiences to be highly creative and innovative:

Creativity is just connecting things. When you ask creative people how they did something, they feel a little guilty because they didn't really do it, they just saw something. It seemed obvious to them after a while. That's because they were able to connect experiences they've had and synthesize new things. And the reason they were able to do that was that they've had more experiences or they have thought more about their experiences than other people. Unfortunately, that's too rare a commodity. A lot of people in our industry haven't had very diverse experiences. So they don't have enough dots to connect, and they end up with very linear solutions without a broad perspective on the problem. The broader one's understanding of the human experience, the better design we will have. (Dunn, 2011)

It is this need to engage in human experiences that drives my desire to see the Aotearoa/New Zealand curriculum extended to equally engage the two governing cultures of this nation, Māori and Western. A balanced curriculum where students are exposed to, and equipped with, more than one knowledge system will enable students to actively participate as citizens of the world (Durie, 2004, p. 2). Acknowledging and discovering connections between world views, knowledge and perceptions of the world can unveil new knowledge that has the potential to benefit societies and future generations (Durie, 2005, pp. 306–09).

In a recent address Sir Mason Durie acknowledged that Māori academics face demanding challenges but also huge opportunities. Māori academics will forever be at the interface of advancing mātauranga Māori (Māori knowledge) and expanding scientific and other research knowledge. For this knowledge to be of greatest impact Durie urges that it be distributed and translated so that people from all walks of life have access to it and can comprehend and apply it. As well as their education communities, Māori academics need to be in constant communication with their whānau, hapū and iwi, business communities and social communities (Gibb, 2012), and engaging in all levels of the social structure within Te Ao Māori and the Western world.

Whakapapa

In my introduction I laid the foundations of 'who I am' in order to contextualise the space and history of my experiences. The term whakapapa often refers to genealogy, which I acknowledged in my introduction. However, whakapapa also means to make layers or foundations ('whaka' – to make, and 'papa'– the ground or layers or foundations). The foundations of how I interact have been from a dual world reality.

Mōhiotanga

Mōhiotanga is knowledge that is derived from experience. What knowledge and qualities have enabled my success in academia thus far? As Jobs highlighted, it is the multitude of experiences and the knowledge that comes from those experiences that enable one's creativity and innovativeness. My mōhiotanga includes those transferable skills mentioned earlier, from my childhood and art education. The skills and knowledge that I have are transferable between various contexts. This includes knowing that nothing is ever complete or finished and creativity is a constant work in progress. Learning to know when to stop is crucial for the success of your creation and your mauri ora (well-being). For example, in art the ultimate stopping point is when the taonga (artwork) has reached the precipice, where the viewer balances between harmony and anxiety, where they are happy to be still and indulge in what they are experiencing while at the same time wanting to step out and take hold of the source. The viewer is experiencing te ihi, te wehi and te wana. Such experience can aid in the restoration and maintenance of one's mauri ora (Kruger, Pitman, Grennell, McDonald, Mariu & Pomare, 2004, p. 15). Learning when to stop or say 'no' is a skill that is transferable. In a work context, it is about knowing about your strengths and weaknesses and knowing when to say 'no'. This saying 'no' is not driven by laziness or ego selfishness; instead it is so that one keeps oneself safe from harm and maintains one's well-being.

This skill, I believe, can only be mastered through trial and error. Trial and errors involves not only getting to that stopping point, but also recognising when you have gone too far. In acknowledging that creativity is constant, I can forgo the pursuit of absolute perfection and instead be satisfied with ensuring that all that I do is with purpose and integrity. These factors instil a sense of humility, which keeps the ego under control, reminding me that the purpose driving my career ambitions is the pursuit of collective mauri ora (wellness) for community well-being. My purpose is driven by the needs of the people and not by my own ego or personal desires. However, through my teaching, personal and management experiences, I have learnt that this includes empowering others. To give others the opportunity to make mistakes and guide them to discover what potential lies within them. It reminds me, as an educator, to 'get out of the way' of learning, in and out of the classroom. Instead, simply pass on the knowledge perceived through my experience and the knowledge gained through theories researched and then let the student evolve their reality and knowledge.

Mātauranga

Mātauranga is the intellectual knowledge derived from research that has been established as factual. The research I have undertaken has been driven by my experiences, wanting to better understand the mainstream tertiary education context and develop a model or system that may provide assistance in developing better understanding of Te Ao Mārama within mainstream education for the benefit of all students. Currently, the model discussed is in its reflective and hypothesising stage of the creative process.

Penetito (2010) describes how since colonisation the purpose of education for Māori people has gone through stages. The first stage saw the assimilating of Māori into mainstream education, which became problematic as education providers were required to be more culturally responsive. The second stage saw Māori developing an alternative for Māori students, kaupapa Māori education. Though kaupapa Māori education is able to fulfill the cultural needs of Māori, Penetito argues that it is funded by the government, therefore has become a mirror image of mainstream education. The third stage enables both mainstream and kaupapa Māori education to weave together while still upholding the integrity and beliefs of both education systems. This is where my research was focused. How is it possible for mainstream and kaupapa Māori education to be integrated and still retain the benefits of both? What I found was that it is not about trying to work within one or the other; it is not about domination but rather collaboration.

In the 1980s Māori artist and art educator Arnold Wilson developed and implemented an art programme called Te Mauri Pakeaka. He talked of 'pakeaka' being the third face or space, which is created when one engages and bridges two worlds or spaces together. Taking Wilson's concept of Te Mauri

Pakeaka, in my research I proposed the third space could be a bicultural space. The development of such a curriculum may be possible by focusing on the similarities between Te Ao Māori and Western art.

From my experience as a tutor I found this most effective when concepts could be transported into varying contexts. This allowed me to reposition ideas and philosophies from Western artists and art movements discussed in lectures and studios into a context that was relevant to Māori students. For example, the use of dichotomies (for example, organised chaos or harmonious discord) is evident in Māori customary art. The kōwhaiwhai (curvilinear patterns) are visually balanced yet are asymmetrical in composition. Art history and mainstream art theory are often problematic for Māori students in that I found Māori students could not locate the purpose or relevance of this knowledge to their art practice. To help students recognise the purpose of the theoretical teachings within the art curriculum, I would pose the following questions and reasoning to the student: What is whakapapa? Is whakapapa important? If yes, why? Art history gives the whakapapa of art. Just as whakapapa lays the foundation of who Māori are as a people and how Māori engage in the world, art history describes how art evolved, what it influenced in the world and how it was influenced. Just as the student may look to their tūpuna for guidance to discover who they are and where they belong, the same can be done with students' art and art practice when they learn art history.

The knowledge I sought and wanted to develop related to how the recontextualising of concepts for Māori students could become more common practice among lecturers and tutors in mainstream education, thereby creating a bicultural curriculum. The concepts of *pakeaka* and *tatau pounamu* became my solution. Identifying that the majority of our educators in mainstream education are of non-Māori descent, I wanted to develop a model that would be user-friendly to this audience. Therefore, to describe the Māori world view, I found non-Māori theorists and educators from mainstream discourse who shared similar concepts and ways of knowing to Te Ao Māori. More specifically, the model is theoretically constructed whereby mātauranga can be expressed, transmitted and shared more appropriately. To advance their understanding of Te Ao Māori, educators would need to actively choose to experience the practices and language within the Māori community by engaging in what is commonly referred to as mōhiotanga.

My new role will give me the opportunity to implement and experiment on how my theory and model could be applied. This role is timely and in an opportune environment. It comes as I complete my master's thesis, so I am ready to put the theory into practice. The government has highlighted that institutions need to improve the educational success levels of Māori and Pasifika students (Ministry of Education, 2010) and AUT promotes that its 'commitment to Māori is shown in its aspiration to be the university of choice for Māori' (AUT University, 2012, p. 5).

Looking back

Māramatanga (enlightenment) arrives when mōhiotanga synthesises with mātauranga and a person is enlightened by the totality of knowledge. It is often punctuated with the 'A-HA!' moments when it all makes sense and an epiphany is experienced. For me this happens when I take the time to reflect on what I have learnt and come to realise why things happened at a particular place and time, and the significant role people play in how I learn and why. It is from these reflections that the knowledge of māramatanga can be passed on so that others' academic journeys may be less hindered and more fluid.

I would like to finish off by sharing a few attributes and life lessons I have learnt to not only survive, but also thrive in the academic arena:

1   Don't be in a hurry. You are not here to move the entire mountain, just to move the rocks that you can.
2   Have a general goal. Be prepared that the path taken may not be the journey you expect. Often you will not reach your goal via the direct route of A to B. Instead you will weave your way through many experiences, collecting knowledge from many people. Your impact will be greater and more beneficial if you accept this.
3   Mentors come in many guises. Respect your tūpuna and those who have paved the way before you. If a senior member of staff is not doing a role in a way you think is effective, realise they may have knowledge you do not yet possess. Sometimes they are being hindered from doing the role effectively. Find out more about them and what they know. What you may realise is that they have information that may ensure that you do not offend anyone or go down the wrong path where you may have to backtrack.
4   Show respect, acknowledge and appreciate opportunities and those who open opportunities up to you. Giving thanks takes only a few seconds and reminds the receiver that they are making a positive difference in someone's life.
5   Endeavours that contribute to meeting the needs of the people and encourage positive change have greater affect.
6   For leadership, do not look to become a leader; instead see what needs to be done and do it.

7   Learn to say no. Know your limits so that you can be of service to your community as long as you can or choose to be. You cannot be everywhere and everything to everyone.

8   Instil balance. You, your family, your community (inclusive of hapū and iwi) and your career are important. When it comes to mauri ora – lead by example.

Much of my journey has occurred during my urban life. I have not yet spent considerable time in the developmental endeavours of my iwi, Ngāti Tūwharetoa and Ngā Puhi. The engagement I have had has been with my hapū, Ngāti Te Maunga. My involvements with Ngāti Te Maunga suggest that they are not yet ready to enter into discussions on education, as their focus has primarily been on the completion of our marae. Therefore, in this instance, I have found my artistic skills to be of greater purpose and need to the people. Feedback from my whānau allows me to keep better informed about what is needed and when. My journey north to Ngā Puhi has not yet begun, although I know it is only a matter of time before my hapū, Ngāti Wharara, may require me to return and to be of service.

What I am conscious of is that I do not currently live in my rohe (tribal lands) and do not want to be seen as the urban coloniser trying to impose change over my whānau. Sustainable changes need to come from those who live in the region. Engagement with my hapū and/or iwi, I believe, will increase as I become better acquainted with the politics and infrastructure of tertiary education. By sharing my knowledge and skills with my iwi, hapū and other communities (local, national and international), I hope to make a conscious contribution in helping to grow a culture of success that enables us all to bask in the uniqueness and empowerment of being Māori. And in this chapter, though my journey started out in art education, it is the transferable skill of creativity that has enabled my journey into academia.

REFERENCES

AUT University (2012). *Auckland University of Technology: Strategic Plan 2012–16.*
    Retrieved from: http://www.aut.ac.nz/about-aut/university-publications

Durie, M. (2004, September). 'Māori achievement: Anticipating the learning environment.'
    Opening keynote address presented at the Hui Taumata Mātauranga IV: Increasing
    Success for Rangatahi in Education. Insight, Reflection and Learning Summit, Taupō/
    Tūrangi, New Zealand.

Durie, M. (2005). 'Indigenous knowledge within a global knowledge system.' In *Higher
    Education Policy, 18*, 301–12. doi: 10.1057/palgrave.hep.8300092.

Gallegos Nava, R. (2012). 'Holistic education, pedagogy of universal love.' Retrieved from:
    http://www.ramongallegos.com/englishversions.htm

Gibb, J. (2012, 1 September). 'Māori academics face future.' *Otago Daily Times*. Retrieved from: http://www.odt.co.nz/campus/university-otago/224077/Māori-academics-face-future

Dunn, J. (2011). 'The key to creativity, according to Steve Jobs.' Retrieved from: http://edudemic.com/2011/10/creativity-steve-jobs/

Kaai, T. (2003). 'Te ao Māori: Māori world view.' Unpublished paper in author's possession, cited with permission.

Kruger, T., Pitman, M., Grennell, D., McDonald, T., Mariu, D. & Pomare, A. (2004). *Transforming Whānau Violence: A conceptual framework* (2nd edn). An updated version of the report from the former Second Māori Taskforce on Whānau Violence. New Zealand Family Violence Clearinghouse/Te Puni Kōkiri.

Manu Ao (2010). 'Manu Ao Academy.' Retrieved from: http://www.manu-ao.ac.nz/

Penetito, W. (2010). 'Māori education: the contribution of kaupapa Māori to mainstream.' Retrieved from: http://webcast.massey.ac.nz/mediasite/Viewer/?peid=a0fe7b04f56e4fac98dbde91060897b51d

Santrock, J.W. (2007). *Child Development* (11th edn). New York, NY: McGraw-Hill.

CHAPTER **12**

Māori Leadership in the Academy: A scientist's perspective

Dan Hikuroa

Introduction

The leadership workshops in 2010 and 2011 organised by the Manu Ao Academy and Ngā Pae o te Māramatanga brought together over 50 Māori, primarily from academia (all New Zealand universities and whare wānanga were represented), which afforded a rare opportunity for the participants to both engage with prominent Māori leaders and also discuss contemporary Māori leadership and Māori academic leadership.

Leadership is a subject to which many have devoted much time and effort. Two current, excellent and relevant examples are the work by Katene (2010) and Williams (2010). Katene (2010) introduces leadership theory and discusses transactional and transformational leadership. He follows with aspects of traditional Māori leadership (for example, rangatira, tohunga and whānau leadership); nineteenth-century aspects (for example, transitioning from transactional to transformational, charismatic and religious-charismatic leadership); twentieth-century aspects with a focus on political leadership; and finally contemporary leadership that encompasses a broad range of skills born out of 'a lifetime negotiating a plural existence in New Zealand' (Katene, 2010, p. 9). Williams (2010) challenges Māori scholars and professionals to consider a seven goal self-reflection framework: objectivity, responsibility, self-confidence, tolerance of ambiguity, learning, balance and action.

This chapter discusses Māori leadership in a contemporary academic context, from my perspective as a scientist living outside my tribal area. The discussion will be guided by the contemporary leadership characteristics discussed in Katene (2010) and the reflective framework in Williams (2010).

Māori in the academy

One of the topics of discussion during the Manu Ao wānanga concerned the concepts of rights and responsibilities. As a virtue of their positions, academics have a suite of rights (for example, remuneration, freedom to think and critique) and consequent responsibilities (for example, teaching, research and service). Māori leadership among academics is impressive and builds upon the legacy of Sir Apirana Ngata and Te Rangi Hīroa Sir Peter Buck with current leaders including Emeritus Professor Sir Mason Durie, Sir Tipene O'Regan, Distinguished Professor Graham Smith, and Professors Linda Smith, Ranginui Walker, Michael Walker, Wally Penetito, Charles Royal, Pare Keiha, Piri Sciascia and Hirini Matunga. These leaders have established a benchmark in the academy for emerging Māori academics to occupy – they created the space for us and they confirmed the right to be there. It is now incumbent upon us, the new and emergent, to fulfil the responsibilities inherent in stepping into that space – to continue to create more space, to train the next generation and to demonstrate we deserve the right to be there.

Two of the recurring themes central to Māori academic leadership that emerged in the Manu Ao wānanga are the role of tikanga and a Māori world view. Effective Māori academic leadership is 'founded on a Māori worldview built on Māori cultural concepts and enacted through tikanga' (Matthews, 2011, p. 3). Two key concepts are whakapapa and pūkenga/tohungatanga (skills/expertise). The responsibilities behind fulfilling and achieving the two concepts are different but inextricably linked: one cannot deny one's whakapapa and if the skills and expertise that an individual possesses are required by the iwi/hapū/whānau then one feels obliged to offer them. This is the minimum expected of everyone. A leader in this context would further be recognised by their standing and reputation in the scientific world and concurrently by their knowledge of whakapapa and tikanga, mātauranga Māori, and demonstrating mōhiotanga (understanding) – in essence they would have dual scholarship. If this is achieved and the individual is recognised as being expert and adept in both Te Ao Māori (the Māori World) and Te Ao Pūtaiao (the Scientific World), and can successfully and easily navigate between the two, they are destined to become, if they are not already, a contemporary academic Māori leader.

Whakapapa

The obligation and responsibility derived from whakapapa was an integral component of traditional Māori society. Although it would be fair to say that it has diminished somewhat since colonisation, increasingly in the past few decades a renaissance of Māori language and culture has resulted in an increased awareness and involvement in affairs at/back home. Key parts of this process are tikanga and mātauranga – they are not only important because they are fundamental, but tikanga can also guide scientists and mātauranga informs scientists. Accordingly, this could give scientists cognisant of tikanga and mātauranga a competitive advantage when exploring new frontiers and can also ground the work in Te Ao Māori – the outcomes of which are then potentially of more relevance to society. In summary, whakapapa provide both opportunity and obligation.

Pūkenga/Tohungatanga

Any scientist in academia must have skills, advanced expertise and the ability to think critically – and Māori scientists are no exception. Therefore Māori scientists in academia have already met the criteria mentioned above – standing and reputation. Increasingly such skills are being required at/back home and many Māori academics are usually well placed to provide the expertise. In addition, Māori academics rarely work in isolation and may be seen as a conduit to further expertise, i.e. those in their research teams, departments, schools, faculties and universities. In summary, Māori scientists in academia possess pūkenga and tohungatanga, and are part of a wider community of experts.

Responsibilities of scientists

I believe scientists need to think more deeply about their social responsibilities. Currently it seems much of the emphasis in science is on the professional responsibility of scientists to adhere to standards agreed upon by the scientific community regarding how research should be conducted (for example, the scientific method, ethics). Such responsibilities can be considered internal. However, scientists also have external social responsibilities concerning the wider community – responsibilities that are often paid little attention. Mark S. Frankel (2013), the director of the Scientific Responsibility, Human Rights and Law Program at the American Association for the Advancement of Science, proposes three core ideas that need to be considered more deeply by scientists:
1. Science is a social institution, with a mission and 'baggage'
2. The global dimension of science
3. Science is the beneficiary of society.

Frankel (2013) posits that 'science is a social institution, with a mission and "baggage" like all other social institutions created by human beings'. There is no denying that all scientists attempt to remain objective while undertaking their research – and many achieve objectivity. However it is equally easy to accept that despite our best and honest attempts, objectivity isn't always reached. I suggest that instead of trying to ignore the obvious, scientists need to discuss and determine their own bias, and the social implications and ramifications of their work, and explore the values and expectations inherent within it.

Appreciation of the global dimension of science has two components. One is being cognisant of the ease by which science is disseminated globally, particularly via the internet. The other relates to understanding that it is the science and, not the scientist, which is the most important. The key reflections outlined by Williams (2010) are pertinent here – objectivity, responsibility, self-confidence, tolerance of ambiguity, learning, balance and action – and I encourage scientists to include these in their approach to science.

Frankel (2013) suggests scientists should be looking beyond themselves and looking to apply their skills to assist with solving societies' problems and realising societies' dreams at all scales – locally, regionally, nationally and globally. Conventionally society has entrusted scientists with the responsibility to determine what questions need to be asked, how they will be answered and how the outcomes will be disseminated.

A challenge and a responsibility for Māori scientists is the need to be accessible and available. Many iwi, hapū or other whakapapa-based organisations talk of a need to grow scientific capability – perhaps another approach to achieve a similar goal is to also 'connect up' capability that exists within the academy. I suggest that Māori scientists, in fulfilling their responsibilities, should be working with Māori communities, to realise their dreams and solve the issues facing Māori communities today. Furthermore, a number of opportunities exist for those who are able to integrate mātauranga Māori and science. An inspection into the commonalities of mātauranga Māori and scientific knowledge is illuminating. Both are bodies of knowledge generated according to methods, contextualised within a world view. A definition of world view is given below:

> Cultures pattern perceptions of reality into conceptualisations of what they perceive reality to be: of what is to be regarded as actual, probable, possible or impossible. These conceptualisations form what is termed the 'world view' of a culture. The World View is the central systemisation of conceptions of reality to which members of its culture assent and from which stems their value system. (Marsden & Henare, cited in Royal 1998, p. 4)

Royal (1998) further posits that the Māori world view was referred to as 'Te Ao Mārama' and it arises out of a 'cosmological whakapapa' which in turn is 'metaphorical of the creation of the world and the psyche of the human being'. Some tentative interpretations he provides of the creation cosmology whakapapa are:

a. *The whakapapa symbolises the passage from ignorance (Te Pō) to knowledge (Te Ao Mārama)*

b. *Knowledge is relative to ignorance*

c. *Knowledge is the descendant of ignorance*

d. *The whakapapa prescribes and describes a distinct pathway which one must follow in order to receive knowledge and particularly to understand (mārama). (Royal, 1998, p. 5)*

Let us now consider science alongside the interpretations of Royal (1998). Science is driven by ignorance, neatly illustrated by Stuart Firestein's (2012) book, *Ignorance: How it drives science.* Undertaking the process of science leads us from a state of ignorance to a state of knowing – akin to the passage from ignorance, Te Pō, to knowledge, Te Ao Mārama. It is also in science that knowledge is relative to and the descendant of ignorance, and that the state of ignorance drives us to attain more knowledge. Furthermore, Royal's final point (quoted above) is that a 'prescribed and distinct pathway' must be followed to receive and understand knowledge. Similarly, scientific knowledge is attained by following the scientific method. It is therefore reasonable to suggest that although mātauranga Māori and science are different, they share some considerable similarities. Māori scientists are therefore very well placed to explore, with Māori communities, the opportunities to be derived from working at the interface between mātauranga Māori and science (cf. Durie, 2004; Peet, 2006; Hikuroa et al., 2011).

Māori in academia

To be successful in academia, Māori scientists are lecturing at high standards and disseminating their findings to the appropriate audiences – primarily by publishing in scientific journals, but increasingly by various methods (reports, presentations, wānanga) to the communities they are working with/for. They are demonstrating pūkenga and tohungatanga. However, the reality for many Māori scientists working in academia is that they live outside their tribal area – referred to variously as rāwaho, taurahere and mātāwaka (Tawhai, 2010). This constitutes a major challenge – despite having many skills (critical thinking, writing) and technical expertise that may be of immense benefit to hapū and iwi, meaningful engagement is hampered by the logistical barrier of distance, compounded by the social barrier of taurahere status. Therefore as this situation has arisen by the application of tikanga, perhaps it is in tikanga that a solution can be found?

Principles, tikanga and leadership

During the three Manu Ao wānanga we were treated to a host of prestigious presenters with amazing messages. I will discuss below only some, particularly those with relevance to the kōrero above.

Professor Charles Royal stated that the ultimate driver – te mea nui – is aroha (love), it inspires, it motivates. By expressing mana aroha we seek to create wholeness in a disjointed world – the deep love flows through the individual and the individual can channel it. He further stated that the potential for rangatiratanga exists in all of us, in the small kindnesses we express in day-to-day activities – he referred to the proverb 'Ahakoa iti, he pounamu' – although it is small, it is pounamu (greenstone), precious. Furthermore, he looked at the component parts of the word 'rangatira' ('ranga' – to bind, to weave; 'tira' – a specific group brought together for a specific purpose, commissioned for a purpose) thus we have rangatira – someone who binds tira together.

Justice Joe Williams discussed tikanga and principles, and while he conceded that there are many, he focused on five he felt were very important. The most important to him is whanaungatanga, kinship. Whanaungatanga embraces whakapapa and relationships (Mead, 2003). In addition, Justice Williams commented that a Māori way of ordering knowledge is based on whakapapa. Another is kaitiakitanga, best translated as guardianship – but the English translation does not adequately capture the concept of kaitiakianga, which itself is derived from mātauranga and manaakitanga.

Justice Williams also discussed mana – mana atua, mana tipuna, mana tangata. In pre-colonisation times, the individual derived much of their mana from mana tipuna – such mana was not guaranteed, but was there to be enhanced or lost, as opposed to being earned outright. An individual with little mana tipuna had a much more difficult time attaining mana, but in many instances did so very successfully by demonstrating tohungatanga, pūkenga, mōhiotanga and rangatiratanga. In contemporary times with a significant number of Māori living as taurahere outside of tribal boundaries, a greater emphasis has been placed on mana tangata than mana tipuna.

Finally he discussed tapu and utu (reciprocity). Tapu is inseparable from mana, from our identity as Māori, from our cultural practices, and is an important element in all tikanga (Mead, 2003). Utu is viewed as the principle of reciprocity in this context, which maintains whanaungatanga. Justice Williams concluded with the comment, 'the sign of the rangatira is to make yourself small, very small, tiny'. A wonderful anecdote, which there are multiple ways to interpret, but the two that struck a chord with me are first, that the rangatira is humble and second, that ultimately they are so successful that they are no longer required. The first interpretation espouses the value placed on humility by Māori and expressed in this whakataukī: 'Waiho mā te tangata e mihi, kia tau ai' – It would be better to let others praise. The second interpretation is twofold – the success of the rangatira is such that the role is now no longer required, and/or they have elevated everyone to the same status.

A key message from Associate Professor Manuka Henare was the concept of Te Ringa Whero – no matter what it is you do, be the best of the best, which brings to mind the pepeha: 'Whāia e koe ki te iti kahurangi; ki te tuohu koe, me maunga teitei' – literally, if you must bow your head, let it be to a lofty mountain, but meaning aim for the stars, for if you should fall short, you will still have reached the moon. To be the best in your discipline can be viewed as tohungatanga.

Associate Professor Merata Kawharu spoke of her experience in the dual role of academic and Māori. One of the concepts she mentioned is 'kanohi kitea' – literally 'the seen face', it also brings with it the idea that the individual is the 'living face' of the ancestors. In practice it means getting 'back home' to get involved – your face ('you') is seen, and you become known. 'Kanohi kitea' has the added benefit of rekindling/establishing friendships and generally strengthening whanaungatanga.

Te Ripowai Higgins engaged with us in a discussion on tikanga, during which she stated that tikanga have changed, that (some) tikanga had to change, and that there are times when tikanga can be 'stretched' – but that it was important to return to the tikanga. An example of when tikanga could be 'stretched' was if it was raining when a visiting group arrived. Typically the pōwhiri would be held outside, but by keeping the visitors outside you were not being a good host, so you could 'stretch' the tikanga to move the pōwhiri inside. However, it is important to understand the tikanga, the 'rules', and their context such that if you chose to break them, it was a conscious decision and you knew why you were breaking them. Of course in the case mentioned above, it is because manaakitanga overrides the tikanga of the pōwhiri. Finally, Mead (2003) states that tikanga are tools of thought and understanding and provide templates and frameworks to guide our actions.

In summary, aroha is the driver, and whanaungatanga, kaitiakitanga, mana, tapu, utu and tikanga are integral, with the last-mentioned subject to pragmatic adherence. Excellence is the ideal and constantly strived for and 'kanohi kitea' is a strategy with the potential to address the issues faced by taurahere.

Conclusion

Māori leaders of tomorrow will be aware of their kinship-based relationship with the environment and of ways in which long-term sustainability of the environment, society, the economy and cultural values can be ensured (Miller, 2005). In order to demonstrate academic leadership an advanced level of proficiency in both Te Ao Pākehā and Te Ao Māori is required. Further leadership is demonstrated by an advanced level of proficiency in science and Te Ao Pūtaiao. I doubt, if asked, whether many Māori scientists in academia would have considered aroha to be a key driver. While I cannot answer for anyone else, my personal driver was always 'to make a positive difference', and when I pondered the question a while, I was able to see that at the core it is aroha that drives wanting to make that difference. Māori scientists in academia, by virtue of their position, have already proven their proficiency in Te Ao Pūtaiao and by enacting the principle of 'kanohi kitea' can whakawhanaungatanga (build effective relationships). In so doing they will be both immersed in mātauranga and kaitiakitanga, which can inform and influence their scientific mahi, and also contributing their technical skills and expertise where required by whānau, hapū and iwi. Furthermore, Māori scientists in academia can act as two-way conduits for other expertise required at/back home and also for rangatahi wanting to enter tertiary education. The challenges facing Māori scientists in the academy are many and demanding, but when overcome in collaboration with their communities can result in significant and potentially transformational outcomes for Māori and therefore New Zealand. Finally, if leadership has been demonstrated in this chapter, it is by action of trying to make a difference, not by intent to be a leader. Mauri ora!

REFERENCES

Durie, M. (2004). 'Exploring the interface between science and indigenous knowledge.' Paper presented at the 5th APEC Research and Development Leaders Forum, 'Capturing Value from Science', Christchurch, New Zealand.

Firestein, S. (2012). *Ignorance: How it drives science.* New York, NY: Oxford University Press.

Frankel, M.S. (2013). 'The social responsibilities of scientists.' Retrieved from: http://sciencecareers.sciencemag.org./career-magazine/previous_issues/articles/2013-02-16/caredit.a1300016

Hikuroa, D., Morgan, K., Durie, M., Henare, M. & Robust, T. (2011). 'Integration of indigenous knowledge and science.' *International Journal of Science in Society, 2,* 7–18.

Katene, S. (2010). 'Modelling Māori leadership: What makes for good leadership.' *MAI Review, 2.* Retrieved from: http://www.review.mai.ac.nz/index.php/MR/article/viewFile/334/477

Marsden, M. & Henare, T. (1992). 'Kaitiakitanga: A definitive introduction to the holistic world view of the Māori.' Unpublished essay. In C. Royal, *Mātauranga Māori: Paradigms and politics*. Report to the Ministry for Research, Science and Technology.

Matthews, N. (2011). 'Reflecting on Māori academic leadership.' *MAI Review, 3*. Retrieved from: http://www.review.mai.ac.nz/index.php/MR/article/view/457/689

Mead, H. (2003). *Tikanga Māori: Living by Māori values*. Wellington, New Zealand: Huia Publishers.

Miller, D.R. (2005). 'Western and Māori values for sustainable development.' In *Proceedings of the Young Māori Leaders Conference 2005*, Wellington, New Zealand.

Peet, J. (2006). 'Systems thinking and common ground.' *International Journal of Transdisciplinary Research 1*(1): 88–99.

Smith, L.T. (1992). 'Ko tāku ko tā te Māori: The dilemma of a Māori academic.' In G.H. Smith & M.K. Hōhepa (eds), *Creating Space in Institutional Settings for Māori*, Monograph no. 15, Research Unit for Māori Education. Auckland, New Zealand: University of Auckland.

Tawhai, V. (2010). 'Rāwaho: In and out of the environmental engagement loop.' In R. Selby, P. Moore & M. Mulholland (eds), *Māori and the Environment: Kaitiaki* (pp. 77–84), Wellington, New Zealand: Huia Publishers.

Williams, L. (2010). 'Leadership: Some underlying processes.' *MAI Review, 2*. Retrieved from: http://www.review.mai.ac.nz/index.php/TK/article/view/388/490

The Challenges of Nurturing Māori Success: Is it my job? Or am I just the 'lecturer'?

Renei Ngawati

Introduction

Kia hiwa rā tātou ngā iwi!
Whāia te mana o ngā tūpuna
Ehara tāku toa i te toa taki tahi, engari taki mano
nō āku tūpuna
Te mana, te wehi, te tapu me te ihi i heke mai ki ahau
nō āku tūpuna
I pepehatia e āku mātua i tohea ai, hei koha rā
Ruiruia taitea, ka tū rā ko taikākā
He tohu rangatira
nō āku tūpuna
Mauri moe, ka mate, mauri tū, mauri ora

Tāku tū, he tū toa
Nō āku tūpuna

(Kingi Ihaka, Wellington Anglican Māori Choir)

The waiata 'Ehara tāku toa' written by Sir Kingi Ihaka is included here to set the context about upholding what is important in order for Māori to progress. This waiata includes whakataukī pertaining to the need for Māori leadership, telling us not only that our success is not of ourselves but of many, but also that signs of leadership are those of strength and perseverance. We require those who are willing to always work hard, use the knowledge of our tūpuna and remember that their work is for the success and sustainability of Māori collectively. If we are not willing to do anything for each other we will die, but if we stand for one another, we live. This comes from the willingness to take the mana of our tūpuna and pass it through to our people. I have included this waiata to illustrate that what we do within our work presently sets a tone for our future and that the motivation for our work as Māori comes from the aspirations of our tūpuna. It is our whakapapa linking our past, present and future that motivates us as Māori to be leaders, teach future leaders and set a pathway for Māori success.

Māori leadership within academia today is still about negotiating a path where our obligations to, and aspirations for, Māori are realised. Why else do we pursue a higher education and then teach our tamariki about the value of attaining education? The Manu Ao academic leadership wānanga in 2010 highlighted that the values of leadership in academia are consistent within and across a range of different contexts. As Māori, we learn this from our experiences, our own culture, our mātua tūpuna, our tamariki. Seemingly, although such cultural knowledge does not leave us in academia, being able to implement this knowledge within academia while maintaining the link with our Māori community is not always easy. The challenge is having a space within an academic environment that allows for our Māori identity to be sustained and nourished.

The academic institution: an environment to foster Māori development

Within the academic institution, the pathway to Māori success and development can be supported in three significant ways: first, by contributing to Māori workforce development by having relevant courses; second, by supporting Māori students to succeed with effective student support systems within tertiary institution; and third, by contributing to research that benefits and enables the building of strong Māori communities. The common aim across all three areas should be the desire to foster Māori development and success. Moreover, being able to achieve and sustain levels of success requires leadership that is effective and people-orientated. This is not to say that Māori staff development initiatives do not exist in academic institutions, but the capacity afforded to enabling academic teaching staff to grow Māori success is not always clearly visible or, indeed, accessible. Māori academic staff need the space, within their roles, to enable the practice of that innate obligation to Māori. This chapter will include a reflection on my experiences that have informed me that academia is no different to other environments where leadership development has been demonstrated as a key ingredient for Māori development. However, balancing and maintaining Māori identity within academia comes with its own set of challenges.

Māori success in academia

Historically, our belief in ourselves as leaders, as achievers and successful contributors to our own people and our wider communities has been compromised through Māori social position, health outcomes, education attainment and wider societal stereotypes about Māori achievement that have hindered young Māori from believing in themselves. We have rangatira past and present who pursued excellence for Māori throughout their lives. Māori leaders like Sir Maui Pomare and Sir Apirana Ngata are celebrated for their achievements, pursuit of education and their work within health, politics and iwi. The struggles they faced, being committed to the betterment of Māori, yet negotiating their priorities for Māori within a Pākehā world, highlight for me their leadership qualities. I take from their histories and achievements that they, along with other Māori leaders before and after them, knew that their work was about Māori success in a changing world.

Their first step to achievement was navigating the Pākehā academic world to obtain an education. This struggle is still going on for us as Māori within the academic world today. Leadership qualities that allow us to survive, learn, develop and achieve within environments that may challenge us exist today as they did then. Whether it is to drive us to succeed, or to help others succeed, there is that inherent obligation to ensure the success of our whakapapa. It is clear from the works of past Māori leaders like Pomare and Ngata that academia is an environment where Māori identity must be nurtured and practised.

Established Māori leaders, both past and present, forged a number of educational pathways that many today are keen to follow when entering into tertiary study. Traditional as well as contemporary Māori leaders often advocated for spaces where Māori could succeed as Māori. This led to a rise in university-based marae, as well as Māori student support systems. Being able to look after each other, and support one another, ultimately increases our chances of succeeding in academia. Across many tertiary institutions today, a number of policies highlight Māori success as a key priority. Equity initiatives, for example, include student support systems while marae and/or Māori student spaces are a common feature in many tertiary settings today. Needing to belong and maintain identity, as well as establishing a sense of whānau away from home – plus knowing how to get from one lecture room to another – are all part of having a successful educational experience.

As an undergraduate I experienced how important it was to look after one another. In 2002, the University of Auckland initiated the Tuakana Programme, to foster second- and third-year student (tuakana) relationships with first-year students (teina). Tuakana were given the role of conducting peer support relationships with teina to help them through the often heavy demands of their first-year study programme(s). The Tuakana Programme helped develop my appreciation of the importance of leadership and relationships between staff and students. It also promoted whanaungatanga within and across different academic departments in the university system. Within an academic environment, where Māori have the lowest education outcomes in comparison to other ethnic groups, providing sustained support for Māori students with programmes like the Tuakana Programme is critical for increasing chances of Māori success (Wells & Te Mātāpuna Māori Students in Psychology, 2006). Of course, leadership approaches to Māori succeeding as Māori in academia are multifaceted and dependent on what motivates individuals to succeed.

Māori development and success: the key ingredients

Emeritus Professor Sir Mason Durie, a leading Māori academic for over 30 years, is a role model for many new and emerging Māori academics. Durie's writings on Māori health promotion have emphasised the need for leadership and capacity building in ways relevant to fostering positive health outcomes for whānau, hapū and iwi. The key determinants for achieving positive health outcomes include political and economic factors, self-determination, iwi capacity building and effective leadership development (Durie, 1997 & 1999; Ratima, 2001). Another common feature of successful Māori-based initiatives is to encourage a strong identity as Māori by including the values of manaakitanga, rangatiratanga, kaitiakitanga and te reo, as well as acknowledging whakapapa. In the following section I reflect on how these values nurtured and developed leadership within two very different environments I have experienced.

Examples of building leadership qualities through Māori identity

Education

I am a former pupil of a Māori bilingual unit at an all-girls school, Kahurangi ki Maungawhau, Auckland Girls' Grammar School. There we learned about the various challenges we would encounter growing up as Māori women. We were given a solid understanding of the importance of becoming future Māori leaders and this helped to define for us our future roles in society more clearly. It was common knowledge to many that developing a sense of pride in oneself was an important characteristic of many of the girls who attended this school. Similarly, the knowledge and understanding of our obligations as wāhine to Māoridom came from our responsibility to care for each other. In my experience, the school was structured very much around tuakana–teina (older–younger) relationships that supported succeeding as wāhine Māori.

Sport

Māori participation in sport is often a vehicle used for Māori development (Ngawati, Ngawati & Paenga, 2008). Touch rugby has always had a high participation rate of Māori (Sport and Recreation New Zealand, 2002) and this provided the opportunity to incorporate traditional cultural values and practices into the development of Māori Touch New Zealand, an autonomous Māori sports organisation established in 1998. My whānau has been involved in touch since it became an established sport in 1989. Through observing my parents and other whānau, I have come to understand that leadership and culture are transferable, relational and based on establishing positive relationships. Examples of leadership observed in sport can be readily adopted and adapted for application in academic settings. At the iwi level, Māori Touch New Zealand has structured itself to represent iwi priorities. Māori Touch New Zealand's principles, for example, include rangatiratanga, manaakitanga, kaitiakitanga, ōritetanga (doing what is right) and whakapapa, and were determined by iwi members. The qualities of leadership that have contributed to the success of Māori Touch New Zealand relate to maintaining the core values of Māori whānau.

Implementing the ingredients to success within the lecturer's role

One of the benefits of teaching within academia is seeing the students that I have taught graduate. Participating in Māori student achievement initiatives within the university has allowed me to see their growth. It has also assisted my growth as a lecturer. Experiencing the establishment of Māori student study spaces and tuakana–teina mentoring programmes, catering for the learning needs of Māori, and an annual Māori health student graduation has led me to appreciate the growth of AUT University over these recent years.

I teach health papers aimed at informing students from various study disciplines about the issues surrounding the health status of Māori and factors needed for equitable health outcomes. I strive to show them that improving Māori health outcomes is not limited to our health system, but the wider factors such as education, effective social policy, iwi participation in all levels of society, partnership, whānau realising their full potential, strong Māori identity and leadership. I show them that the terms whakapapa, mana, rangatiratanga, whānau, hapū and iwi are all vital values for Māori development. These values are the stepping stones for Māori to emerge as leaders within their communities, to take charge of what is important to them and navigate their worlds in order to achieve. This is what I teach, while struggling myself to have these values guide my role as an emerging Māori academic.

To put this into context, I have experienced working within Māori academic departments and appreciate the space for Māori staff to work with Māori development as a strategic aim. I am not, however, currently based within a Māori academic department, nor do I have a whānau of Māori colleagues working alongside me. I feel less able within this contrasting environment to contribute to, or practise in a way that supports, Māori development. This may not be the case for other Māori staff within a university role, but I feel this is a risk for Māori academic staff who sit alone within their schools or departments. Māori teaching staff need to have a place within their academic institutes where their own culture and tikanga are fully integrated and respected, where they can practise what research, Māori communities, and our history all say will empower Māori to succeed.

The academic's pathway within the academic institute mainly consists of research outputs and teaching commitments. Māori academics predominantly focused on research have the opportunity to research and disseminate Māori knowledge they have acquired through their research activities and involvement in Māori communities. Academic research provides an avenue to develop pathways for Māori development. This has been assisted by the emergence of Kaupapa Māori theory in 1997, which validated the recognition and practice of tikanga Māori in traditional mainstream academic institutions for the first time (Smith, 1999). Māori and Indigenous research centres (e.g. Ngā Pae o te Māramatanga, University of Auckland) and wānanga (Te Wānanga o Raukawa, Te Wānanga o Aotearoa and Te Whare Wānanga o Awanuiārangi) have become spaces that have not only enhanced Māori contributions to academia but have enabled the aspirations of Māori communities to flourish. The ability for Māori to be change agents in their own communities has become the mantra for taking back control of their educational futures.

As a university lecturer more focused on teaching, there is not such a clear pathway for supporting Māori aspirations. How do I navigate my role as a lecturer and my responsibilities as a Māori? My identity tells me that the growth of Māori comes from nurturing the whakapapa on which our culture and knowledge is built. My identity tells me that the connection and practice of whanaungatanga is a key component to survival and development. This contrasts with my experience of being one of many Māori staff in an academic institution but the only Māori teaching staff member in a department. The physical isolation from each other, I believe, comes to be reflected in an isolation from the reasons we are in the positions – for the success and achievement of Māori. In no way am I saying that nothing is being done about this within the university system, but from my perspective our leaders within our institutes, Māori and non-Māori, could better connect the mahi of academic and allied staff. There is a need for a clear affirmation within the academic environment that 'looking after Māori development' is required within the job description. My connection with the Māori workforce and wider community comes from my belief in the necessity for that link between academia and Māori communities in order to ensure that students learn the ingredients for Māori success. A disconnection between Māori academic staff, Māori students and Māori communities because of an obligation to only teach and research is unacceptable. This, in my view, is not leadership, nor is it fulfilling my innate obligation to my people, or respecting my whakapapa.

This chapter has discussed the idea that the factors for leadership for Māori within academia are no different to what are needed in any other environment where we strive to succeed. We may face many challenges that hinder our ability to implement these factors in tertiary institutes, but having the space as academic staff to always be involved and contribute to Māori success is vital, not only for the development of ourselves, as Māori academics, but also for the students and other staff within the institute. Debating, negotiating, arguing and finding support systems for our needs as Māori within academia has been a long battle. Arguing to ensure that the factors of Māori success are implemented within our jobs as academic staff is a tough battle, but deeply necessary. Those who have succeeded and have become well-established Māori academics are those who have found a way to navigate through the bureaucracies and politics inherent in institutions, implementing what is important for Māori development, while at the same time staying true to the vision for Māori success. I admire these leaders. Due to them, Māori staff across all disciplines are encouraged as part of their professional role to be involved in supporting, where they can, a wider vision of Māori success for future generations.

From my own experiences, I know that keeping the idea of 'whakapapa' as the driving force behind the work that we do as Māori opens the gateway for success. It's within our communities. It's in any environment. Navigating Māori development built on the value of whakapapa takes leadership. It is our connection to our tūpuna and our histories that tell us we need to be connected to one another for the development of our future leaders. We need that balance and link between our past that drives us, the present in which we do the work and the future where the fruits of that work are realised.

At the Manu Ao Academy wānanga I was grateful to hear that the learning and discussion about Māori academic leadership development was about the lessons that we learn from our whānau and our tūpuna. That what drives us as Māori academics is about what makes us Māori – our whakapapa. The leadership that is demonstrated within an academic environment is not just research outputs or teaching requirements. It is about knowing how to navigate our way through an academic environment that does not compromise the very reasons why we are there as Māori. Navigation between the aspirations of Māori and the academic system to realise full Māori potential is the goal. Our past Māori leaders had to navigate that academic system and we as Māori are still doing that today. They paved a way for us and it is our responsibility to keep navigating. To stand isolated and have a voice justifying the need to implement factors within a teaching role requires a strong connection with others within the institute and the community. To not stand, navigate and challenge the status quo of the academic role is to not adhere to the words of my tūpuna: 'Tāku tū, he tū toa. Nō aku tūpuna.' I stand as a leader, passed down from my ancestors.

REFERENCES

Durie, M. (1997). 'Whānau, whanaungatanga and healthy Māori development.' In P. Te Whaiti, M.B. McCarthy & A. Durie (eds), *Mai i Rangiātea: Māori wellbeing and development* (pp. 16–19). Auckland, New Zealand: Auckland University Press and Bridget Williams Books.

Durie, M. (1999). 'Te Pae Māhutonga: A model for Māori health promotion.' *Health Promotion Forum of New Zealand Newsletter*, 49, 2–5.

Mayer, A., Wilson, N., Signal, L. & Thompson, G. (2006). 'Patterns of sports sponsorship by gambling, alcohol and food companies: an internet survey.' *BMC Public Health*, 6, 95.

Ngawati, C., Ngawati, R. & Paenga, M. (2008). 'Indigenous partnership strategies in sport: Māori Touch as a vehicle for traditional knowledge and well-being and whānau/hapu/iwi development.' Paper presented at the Traditional Knowledge Conference 2008, Traditional knowledge and gateways to balanced relationships, University of Auckland, Auckland.

Ratima, M. (2001). 'Kia uruuru mai a hauora: being healthy, being Māori, conceptualising Māori health promotion.' PhD thesis, University of Otago, Dunedin, New Zealand.

Smith, L.T. (2012). *Decolonizing Methodologies: Research and indigenous peoples.* Dunedin, New Zealand: University of Otago Press/Zed Books.

Sport and Recreation New Zealand (2002). 'Push play facts, II.' Wellington, New Zealand: Sport and Recreation New Zealand.

Wells, M. & Te Mātāpuna Māori Students in Psychology (2006). 'SSG psychology tuakana programme.' Faculty of Science, University of Auckland, Auckland.

Notes

1 For a fuller account of this development see Reilly, M.P.J. (2011), 'The beginnings of Māori Studies within New Zealand universities', *He Pūkenga Kōrero: A Journal of Māori Studies 10*(2), 4–9.

2 This was first coined by Isaac Featherston in 1856 (King, 1997, p. 38) and supported by the drop in Māori population of approximately 60,000 people in a period of less than one hundred years following the signing of the Treaty.

3 Professor Michael Walker (Whakatōhea) is an internationally renowned scientist who has systematically characterised the animal navigational system that uses the earth's magnetic field. He also established the award-winning School of Biological Sciences Tuākana Programme at the University of Auckland, an academic support programme for Māori and Pasifika students, which after 21 years is still going strong. Professor Walker and Professor Linda Tuhiwai Smith were the inaugural co-directors of Ngā Pae o te Māramatanga, New Zealand's Māori Centre of Research Excellence.

4 Professor Linda Tuhiwai Smith (Ngāti Awa, Ngāti Porou) is a world leader in Indigenous education, health and ethics. Her seminal text *Decolonizing Methodologies: Research and Indigenous Peoples* has been cited more than 5000 times and is considered to have transformed the ways that research is conducted in and with Indigenous communities. In collaboration with her husband Professor Graham Hingangaroa Smith, she pioneered Kaupapa Māori methodologies and established the successful MAI doctoral programme which facilitated 500 Māori to complete their doctorates over a five-year period.

5 Professor Richard Faull (Te Āti Awa) is a prominent neuroanatomist whose cutting-edge research has changed the classification of Huntington's disease symptomology and pathology. He has also systematically characterised several novel pathways of neurogenesis (birth of new brain cells) in the human brain. Professor Faull's work is highly regarded internationally and he is widely considered to be New Zealand's most influential neuroscientist.

6 Professor Karina Walters (Choctaw Nation of Oklahoma) is a world leader in American Indian and Alaska Native health, historical trauma and mental health. She has led several groundbreaking studies associated with health-risk outcomes in American Indian communities. Professor Walters founded and directs the interdisciplinary Indigenous Wellness Research Institute (IWRI) at the University of Washington.

7 Associate Professor Manulani Aluli Meyer (Native Hawaiian from Hilo, Wailuku) is world renowned for her research on Indigenous education and philosophy. Her work exploring Hawaiian epistemology through land, people, history and aspirations is highly regarded. She is currently the International Indigenous Professor at Te Wānanga o Aotearoa.

8 What is the most important thing in the world? The people! The people! The people!

9 The literal meaning is 'the pigeon coos, the kākā screeches'. Metaphorically this is about each person having their own voice and being their own person.

10 Māori deities; the children of Ranginui and Papatūānuku are the departmental gods of the Māori world.

11 Whakakī Lake is part of a coastal lagoon system. The PCE report focused on management of the entire system not just the lake.

12 In this context whenua refers to lands, waters and natural resources, and spiritual and cultural elements such as tūrangawaewae (place to stand, rights of residency) and mana whenua (tribal authority, power from the land).

13 For a more detailed discussion of the effects of colonisation of the landscape on the Whakakī Lake ecosystem see Coombes and Hill (2005) and PCE reports (1993a, 1993b).

14 The phrase 'remnant wetlands' is a reference to wetland ecosystems that have been transformed often by drainage and agricultural activities and are a mere reflection of the original system.

15 The two main owners of the lake property are Whakakī Lake Trust (lower end of lake) and Whakakī 2N Incorporation (upper end of lake).

16 Information on the restoration work of the Whakakī Lake Trust can be found on the Ngā Whenua Rāhui website http://www.doc.govt.nz/getting-involved/landowners/nga-whenua-rahui/nga-whenua-rahui-fund/featured-projects/whakaki

17 Retrieved from http://www.Māori.org.nz/tikanga/default.php?pid=sp100&parent=95

18 From which 'pedagogy' is derived.

19 Powell (2010, p. 78) refers to the West Semitic languages generally, including 'Phoenician, Hebrew … Aramaic … [and] the modern Arabic script[s]'. Havelock (1980) refers only to Phoenician.

20 For example, Bano (2012) states, 'between 1066 and 1190 … all school masters in England … were trained in foreign schools' (p. 30).

21 Oxford, like Cambridge, maintained its religious loyalties through multiple methods, including religious testing. Until 1886 (Salter & Lobel, 1954), the institution required all students 'to subscribe on matriculation to the Thirty-Nine Articles' of Religion, the doctrines of the Church of England (Anderson, 2006, p. 26).

22 Reporting on Oxbridge elitism (Bolton, 2012) continues.

Contributors' biographies

Dr James Ataria (Rongomaiwahine, Ngāti Kahungunu, Ngāti Tūwharetoa) is a Senior Lecturer in the Ecology Department, Agricultural and Life Sciences Faculty, Lincoln University, Christchurch, New Zealand. He is also an ecotoxicologist for the Cawthron Institute and a member of the Māori Advisory Committee for the Environmental Protection Authority.

Dr Amohia Boulton (Ngāti Ranginui, Ngāi Te Rangi, Ngāti Pūkenga) is a Senior Researcher at Whakauae Research for Māori Health and Development. Amohia works on health services research, specifically the relationship between, and contribution of, government policy, contracting mechanisms, performance monitoring and accountability frameworks in improving health outcomes for Māori.

Dr Melanie Cheung (Ngāti Rangitihi, Te Arawa) is a Postdoctoral Research Fellow at the University of Waikato. Melanie is committed to exploring both Indigenous and Western scientific paradigms in her work, which integrates experimental neuroscience, bioethics, tikanga and mātauranga Māori to help people with neurodegenerative diseases.

Piki Diamond (Ngā Puhi, Ngāti Tūwharetoa) is a Teaching & Learning Consultant in the Centre for Learning & Teaching and is currently completing her Master of Arts degree in Māori Development at Auckland University of Technology (AUT).

Dr Margaret Forster (Rongomaiwahine, Ngāti Kahungunu) is a Lecturer in Massey University's Te Pūtahi-a-Toi and teaches about the management of natural resources and adaptation and resilience of culture.

Dr Heather Gifford (Ngāti Hauiti, Te Āti Haunui-a-Pāpārangi) is Director of Whakauae Research for Māori Health and Development. Her research focuses on Indigenous public health research, in particular tobacco control with a focus on prevention and policy, health service delivery and intervention research.

Dr Marewa Glover (Ngā Puhi) is Director of the University of Auckland's Centre for Tobacco Control Research and Co-Director of New Zealand's Tobacco Control Research Tūranga: a programme informing how to achieve a smoke-free nation by 2025. Marewa has led and assisted numerous studies into smoking and other Māori health kaupapa over the last 17 years.

Katarina Gray-Sharp (Ngāti Rangi, Ngāti Kauwhata, Ngāti Raukawa ki te Tonga, Ngāti Rangiwēwehi) is a Teaching Consultant with Massey University's National Centre for Teaching and Learning. Katarina's work on kāinga and tino rangatiratanga in housing policy is part of her co-edited set text (2011). Previous research includes mana wāhine methodology, m-learning, and whānau health. Currently, she is a daily Twitter user (@TeachingConsult) interested in somatic knowledge and alterity.

Meegan Hall (Ngāti Ranginui, Ngāi Te Rangi, Ngāti Tūwharetoa, Tainui) is Associate Dean, Learning and Teaching (Poukairangi Ako) for Toihuarewa and a Lecturer in Academic Development in the Centre for Academic Development at Victoria University of Wellington. She works with Māori and Pasifika academic staff, encourages culturally responsive teaching and learning practices for Māori and Pasifika students, and teaches on the Postgraduate Diploma in Higher Education Learning and Teaching (PHELT) programme and Orientation Programme for New Academics. Her primary research area is Māori academic development and she publishes on Māori academic practice, Māori pedagogies, and Māori student achievement in higher education.

Dr Dan Hikuroa (Tainui and Te Arawa) is a Research Director for Ngā Pae o te Māramatanga based at the University of Auckland. Dan is an Earth System Scientist with an interest in the integration of mātauranga (Māori knowledge) and science.

Dr Simon Lambert (Ngāti Ruapani ki Waikaremoana, Tūhoe) is a Lecturer in Māori Environmental Planning and Development at Lincoln University, Christchurch, New Zealand. Simon specialises in Indigenous development issues, including small-scale Māori horticulture, customary fisheries, Māori farming history and modern Indigenous agribusiness. He is currently researching the Indigenous geography of hazards and disasters, with particular interest in urban Indigenous resilience.

Melanie Mark-Shadbolt (Ngāti Kahungunu ki Wairarapa, Ngāti Porou, Ngāti Raukawa, Te Arawa) works for the Bio-Protection Research Centre at Lincoln University, Christchurch, New Zealand as the Māori Research & Development Coordinator and Māori Bioprotection Theme Leader. Her research focuses on Indigenous development, leadership and people, community engagement and disaster management.

Dr Nathan Matthews (Ngāti Toki, Te Hikutū ki Ngā Puhi) is a Senior Lecturer in Māori Education in the Institute of Education at Massey University, where he teaches on Māori leadership in education, cultural difference in education and engaging whānau in education. His research interests centre around Māori education, particularly Māori boys' education, and the relationship between culture, religion and education.

Renei Ngawati (Ngāti Hine (Ngāti Te Ara/Ngāti Kōpaki), Ngā Puhi, Ngāti Porou (Te Aitanga-a-Hauiti)) is a Lecturer in Māori Health and Development at AUT University. Renei has been involved in iwi development through whānau involvement in sport, education and health initiatives in urban and rural Māori communities. She is pursuing a Master of Public Health focusing on how sport is used as a vehicle for Indigenous development.

Pip Pehi's passions and kaupapa stem from aroha, whenua and wairua and aim to assist people to remember our connections and responsibilities to Papatūānuku, ourselves, our whānau and communities. Pip's home is in the Hokianga where she lives to be of service to tupuna, whenua and people. Her academic qualifications include a PhD (Social Psychology) and Diploma in Clinical Psychology from the University of Otago.

Dr Reremoana F. Theodore (Ngā Puhi) is a Research Fellow at the Dunedin Multi-disciplinary Health and Development Research Unit and the National Centre for Lifecourse Research at the University of Otago. Her interests include life course research, child and youth health and development, and Māori health.

Dr Paul Whitinui (Ngā Puhi, Te Aupōuri, Ngāti Kurī) is an Associate Professor of Māori Teacher Education at the University of Otago College of Education (Te Kura Ākau Taitoka). Paul's current role involves providing professional and strategic leadership in the area of Māori teacher education and employing culturally responsive pedagogies and practices. His research interests are broadly linked by relationships between Māori and Indigenous teacher education, Indigenous knowledge, whānau resiliency and Indigenous health.

Glossary

Aotearoa me Te Waipounamu New Zealand
aroha to love, have affection, feel concern for, feel compassion for, empathise
atawhai kindness
atua deity, deities
awa river(s)
hapū sub-tribe
hui meeting
iwi tribe
kai food
kaikaranga female elder who has the ceremonial role of calling people onto the marae in the pōwhiri
kaikōrero formal speaker during the pōwhiri
kaitiakitanga stewardship, guardianship, customary practices associated with caring for and looking after the environment
karakia prayer, especially to open and close meetings
katakata to laugh, be humorous
kaumātua tribal elder(s), male elder(s)
kaupapa topic
kawa protocol
kotahitanga unity
kuia female elder(s)
mahi toi art practice
mana honour, integrity, prestige, status
mana whenua territorial rights
manaaki to care for, to support others
manaakitanga culture of caring for others
marae focal point of the Māori community, sacred tribal gathering place, courtyard in front of the meeting house
mātauranga knowledge
mātua tūpuna ancestors
maunga mountain
mihi formal and informal greetings
mihi whakatau formal welcome
moana ocean
mōhiotanga understanding
mōteatea chant
motu island, nation
noa to be free from tapu, to be ordinary and unrestricted
ōritetanga doing what is right
Papatūānuku Earth Mother
pepeha proverbial sayings
pono to be true, valid, honest

pōwhiri traditional formal welcoming ceremony

pūkenga skills

rangatira chief, leader

rangatiratanga leadership, self-determination

Ranginui Sky Father

Tā Sir

take issue at hand

tamariki children

tangata whenua people of the land

taonga treasure, artwork

taonga tuku iho gifts handed down from the ancestors, treasures

tapu sacred, restricted

Te Ao Māori the Māori World

Te Ao Mārama the World of Enlightenment

Te Ao Pūtaiao the Scientific World

te ihi magnetism

te reo (Māori) language

te wehi awe and fear

te wana inspiration

teina younger sibling of the same gender

tiaki to protect, to look after

tika to be right, appropriate, correct, straight, direct, just, fair

tikanga customary practices or ceremonies

tipuna/tupuna ancestor

tīpuna/tūpuna ancestors

tohungatanga expertise

tuakana–teina senior–junior relationship

tūrangawaewae place to stand, place where one has rights of residence and belonging through kinship and whakapapa

ūkaipō place that nourishes our essence

urupā cemetery

waiata song

wānanga learning session

wero challenge

whaikōrero speeches

whakaaetanga acceptance

whakapaitia approval

whakapapa lineage, genealogy, genealogical links; to establish a genealogical connection

whakataukī, whakatauākī proverbial sayings

whakawhanaungatanga getting to know others

whānau family, extended family

whanaungatanga relationships, kinship; it incorporates specific responsibilities towards whānau

wharenui meeting house

whenua land

Index

University of Otago 83, 90
University of Waikato 90, 165
utu (reciprocity) 20, 42, 64, 151

values, see leadership values
Victoria University 24, 130
visitors, guests, see manaakitanga
vocational training 129, 156

waiata 155
Wairoa District Council 116
wairua, wairuatanga (spirituality) 34,
43, 94, 105, 106, 123, 128
Walker, Professor Michael 77, 78, 147
Walker, Professor Ranginui 147
Walters, Karina 77
Wānanga o Aotearoa, Te 160
Wānanga o Raukawa, Te 160
wānanga, see Manu Ao, University
wetlands, see Whakakī Lagoon
Williams, Justice Joe 23, 151

Williams, Professor Les 43, 90, 146
Wilson, Arnold 141

whānauā 136
whakairoā 23, 85, 87, 139
Whakakī Lagoon 112–20; Lake
Trust 116, 117, 119
whakapapa 58, 94, 122, 128, 140, 147,
150, 161
whakapapa, Maui Igorovitch Thung 40
Whakatāne 89
whakataukī 20, 31, 33, 34, 42, 46, 52, 79,
80, 91, 103, 151, 152, 155
Whakauae Research for Māori Health
and Development 53, 165
whānau 50, 84, 103, 123–24
Whānau Ora 37
whanaungatanga: in academia 51, 85,
158; principle 43, 51, 81, 93, 136,
153, 160
Whitinui, Kainamu 95